ENCLOSURE, ENVIRONMENT & LANDSCAPE

IN SOUTHERN ENGLAND

ENCLOSURE, ENVIRONMENT & LANDSCAPE

IN SOUTHERN ENGLAND

John Chapman & Sylvia Seeliger

TEMPUS

First published 2001

PUBLISHED IN THE UNITED KINGDOM BY:

Tempus Publishing Ltd
The Mill, Brimscombe Port
Stroud, Gloucestershire GL5 2QG

PUBLISHED IN THE UNITED STATES OF AMERICA BY:

Tempus Publishing Inc.
2 Cumberland Street
Charleston, SC 29401
(Tel: 1-888-313-2665)

Tempus books are available in France and Germany
from the following addresses:

Tempus Publishing Group   Tempus Publishing Group
21 Avenue de la République   Gustav-Adolf-Straße 3
37300 Joué-lès-Tours   99084 Erfurt
FRANCE   GERMANY

British Library Cataloguing in Publication Data.
A catalogue record for this book is available from the British Library.

ISBN 0 7524 2079 8

Typesetting and origination by Tempus Publishing.
PRINTED AND BOUND IN GREAT BRITAIN.

Contents

Acknowledgements

We would like to express our gratitude to the Economic and Social Research Council and to the Leverhulme Trust, who each funded part of the research upon which the book is based. Our thanks are also due to the archivists and staff of the five county record offices, and of Portsmouth City Record Office for their patient help in tracking down the (often obscure) records involved, and to the staff of the Public Record Office for their help with the nationally held documentation.

We are grateful also to the various owners of private record collections who allowed us access, notably Queen's College, Oxford, Corpus Christi College, Oxford, New College, Oxford, the Arundel Castle Estate, Longleat Archives, Winchester College and Winchester Cathedral Archives.

Professor Michael Turner kindly provided copies of his draft lists of failed enclosure bills, and Bill Johnson, of the University of Portsmouth Cartographic Unit, drew the maps. Paul Carter digitised the county boundaries, and Dr Alastair Pearson made available the digitised versions of the North Hayling and Portsmouth tithe maps, on which maps 2 and 35 are based.

To all of these, and to the many colleagues and others who have helped, encouraged and offered comment over a very long-drawn-out project, we would like to offer our thanks.

Lastly, special thanks to Polly Chapman for her invaluable support. Her help with the data collection was much appreciated, and she undertook the unenviable task of reading through the entire text. Her sharp eye for ambiguities and for contortions of English style enabled many to be removed. Any which remain are, of course, the sole responsibility of the authors.

List of illustrations

1

Introduction

Over the last twenty years or so, interest in the rural landscape has grown enormously. As the vast changes which have taken place in farming have in turn brought changes to the landscape, there has been an increasing awareness that much-valued features of the rural scene are under threat of disappearance. The loss of hedgerows and woodlands, heathlands and moorlands has brought growing demands for their preservation, as features which are both aesthetically pleasing and a part of the essential Englishness of the rural scene. These landscapes, however, are themselves a product of past changes wrought by human beings, and many owe their character to another period of profound upheaval: the enclosure movement of the eighteenth and nineteenth centuries. It is with the impact of this movement on the four central south-coast counties of Wiltshire, Dorset, Hampshire and Sussex that this book is concerned.

At the beginning of the eighteenth century a large part of the arable land of the four counties lay in open fields, and the overwhelming majority of parishes possessed some form of communal pasture or waste (see Fig. 1). By 1900, almost all the former had disappeared, while the latter had gone from many parishes and been drastically reduced in many of the rest. Most of this land, whether arable or pasture, was both 'open' and 'common' in 1700. In legal theory, the distinction between these two terms was of great significance, for land which was '*open*' (without fences or other physical divisions between properties) was not necessarily '*common*' (subject to common rights or communal control) and *vice versa*. Land which was merely open could be enclosed at will by the owners, whereas land which was common could not. Hence, as Joan Thirsk (1967, pp. ix-x) has stressed, there is a need for care and precision in using terms like 'common fields' and 'open fields', for they are not interchangeable. In this book, '*open*' has been used as a general term, while '*common*' has been reserved for cases where rights are known to have existed, or where documents specifically refer to land in this way.

In practice, these distinctions are often blurred. Fields which were undoubtedly common at one time might see their common rights gradually fall into disuse, and might slip almost imperceptibly into mere *open* fields; precisely when one became the other is almost impossible to pinpoint with any accuracy. Even contemporaries were not always sure, for the fact that rights had ceased to be exercised did not necessarily mean that they had legally ceased to exist. Wrangles over the precise status of a piece of land were a

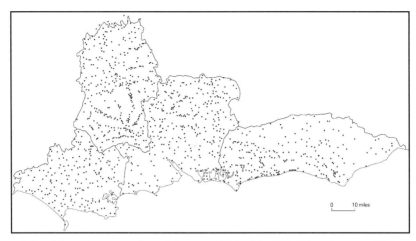

1. Localities with any type of recorded commonable land in 1700. Those shown outside the boundaries are believed to have had some land within the historic counties.

source of much acrimonious dispute throughout the two centuries. Adding to the confusion was the fact that the law itself was not entirely clear about whether 'common fields' were genuinely common in the legal sense, as will be discussed later.[1] If they were not, then any individual could withdraw his or her land from the system at will, and no formal enclosure of any sort would be necessary.

In these circumstances, it is hardly surprising that enclosure was an untidy, confused and often disputatious process. Legally speaking, the term 'enclosure' (or 'inclosure' as it was normally spelt in the eighteenth and early nineteenth centuries) was the process whereby any common rights over a piece of land were abolished and the land divided amongst the proprietors, to be held *'in severalty'*, in other words in individual ownership unfettered by communal constraints. It did not necessarily imply that the land concerned would be fenced or hedged, though in practice this was the result in the great majority of cases. As has been stated, a formal act or agreement was not necessary if land was merely open. In practice one was often used, either to overcome any of the doubts mentioned earlier about the real status of such land, or to facilitate the exchanges of land which often took place between the owners. Characteristically, the property of any individual in the open fields was highly fragmented into a number of tiny, widely scattered plots (see map 2), and consolidation of these into one or two much larger blocks was a principal objective of many of those advocating change. A formal enclosure normally appointed referees or commissioners to carry out this reorganisation process, and could be used as well to provide a legal record of any private exchanges agreed between specific individuals. An enclosure might thus affect a good deal more than just the common or even open land of a manor or township.

Enclosure could be achieved in a number of different ways, and the legal technicalities of the various methods are discussed at length in Gonner's detailed study from the early part of this century (Gonner, 1912, pp. 4-29). From the point of view

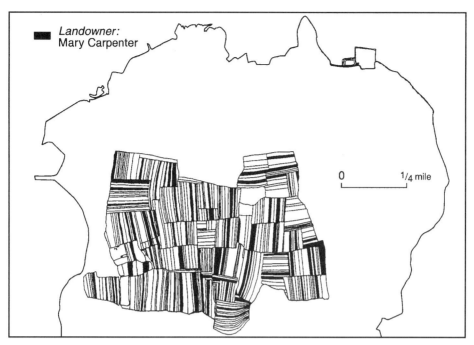

2. An example of fragmented ownership in open fields: North Hayling fields prior to enclosure.

of the practical effects, however, it is sufficient to distinguish four main methods, which may be described, in ascending order of formality and legal status, as: piecemeal enclosure; unity of possession; formal agreement; and parliamentary enclosure. A fuller discussion of these methods and their implications is contained in Chapter 2, but they may be briefly distinguished as follows. *Piecemeal enclosure*, as its name implies, involved uncoordinated individual action to remove parts of the field or common from communal use; *unity of possession* occurred when one individual succeeded in acquiring all the land and rights in it; *formal agreement*, as defined here, consisted of a properly drawn up and signed arrangement amongst all the parties to enclose a specified piece of land; finally, *parliamentary enclosure* involved either the passing of an individual act, or an award under the authority of one of the general enclosure acts passed in the course of the nineteenth century.

Enclosure by the first two means was a very long established process, which can be traced back at least into the early Middle Ages. A major enclosure movement in the fifteenth century and the early years of the Tudor period had created considerable social unrest, and had resulted in a substantial body of legislation aimed especially at restraining those seeking to achieve unity of possession in order to enclose (Beresford and Hurst, 1971). Enclosure by formal agreement was certainly in use in the Tudor period, but it did not become common until the seventeenth century, by which time the first enclosure acts began to appear. However, there were a mere six enclosures by Act of Parliament in the whole of the century, and all of these are highly untypical, if indeed they should be regarded as enclosure acts at all. The only one affecting the counties under consideration was the earliest of all, that for Radipole in Dorset in 1603, but as this merely allowed the enclosure of a small piece of common for the building of a chapel, its status as an enclosure in the normal sense of the word must be regarded as doubtful. If we follow instead the definition of the great eighteenth-century agricultural writer Arthur Young and regard the enclosure of Ropley (Hampshire) in 1709 as the first true enclosure, then this book may be regarded as covering the period of parliamentary enclosure in these counties (Young, 1808, p. 55).

It must be emphasised that the choice of this particular time period is in no way intended to reinforce the view that the history of enclosure in the eighteenth and nineteenth centuries can be equated with parliamentary enclosure. Though most authorities accept that other forms of enclosure occurred in the years immediately following 1700, the orthodox view is that at least by about 1760 these had been largely replaced by the the use of Acts of Parliament (See, for example, Turner, 1980, p. 58, or Clark, 1998, p. 92). The inevitable corollary of this is that, with a few minor exceptions, anything which was not enclosed by parliamentary action after that date and was not still open in the twentieth century must have been enclosed at some earlier period. As will be demonstrated later, this is certainly not valid for the central southern counties. Within this area, there is ample evidence that other forms of enclosure persisted on a significant scale alongside those by act, and were still being used in the late nineteenth century. It is the aim of this book to examine the part played by all these methods of enclosure during the period, and to assess the impact of each on the landscape and environment.

Much of this overemphasis on parliamentary enclosure derives from the fascination of so many researchers with the counties of the English Midlands. Intensive studies, from pioneering workers like Hunt (1955) to more recent writers, for example Turner (1973) and Neeson (1978), have revealed a great deal about the nature of the movement in counties such as Leicestershire and Northamptonshire, and there has been a tendency for these findings to become accepted as typical of the country as a whole. In fact, enclosure during the eighteenth and nineteenth centuries shows enormous variation from one region to another, and there is a strong suggestion of a pattern of continuous change outwards from the centre to the periphery (Chapman, 1987). In other words, Leicestershire and Northamptonshire form one extreme of the process, while Cornwall, Kent and Cumberland form the other. It would thus seem highly likely that the central southern counties may prove rather closer to the norm than either Northamptonshire or Cornwall. Certainly, as far as parliamentary enclosure is concerned, three of the four counties are far nearer to the national picture in terms of the percentage of land enclosed by this means,[2] and Wiltshire almost exactly matches the national balance between open arable and other types of land (Chapman, 1987).

While the primary aim of this book is to examine the impact of the various types of enclosure on these four specific counties, some of the conclusions may have wider implications. At the very least, it is hoped that, by examining how the enclosure process operated within this area, questions may be raised about the picture at a national level.

2

The Enclosure Process

Before the enclosure process in the central southern counties is examined in detail, it seems appropriate to give some consideration to the general conditions which controlled how and why enclosure took place. It was characteristic of the movement in England that it was always initiated locally and, in consequence, each individual case has its own specific peculiarities of motivation and procedures, but certain general features can be detected which are worthy of discussion.

As has already been suggested, enclosure after 1700 is often seen purely in terms of *parliamentary* enclosure, carried out by individual private acts and concerned with the sweeping away of open field systems. The reality is more complex. Parliamentary enclosure was merely the most obvious and visible aspect of a much larger whole, and the open arable fields were only a part, and often a minor one, of a movement which took huge areas of common downland, common marsh, common woodland and common meadowland and divided it amongst individual landowners to use as they wished. This process was carried out in a wide variety of ways, of varying degrees of formality and legality. At one end of the scale, enclosures by formal agreements, drawn up in proper legal form between all the interested parties, and sometimes subsequently registered with the courts, were in essence little different from those by private act. Like them, they often covered substantial areas of land; like them, they often appointed independent commissioners and surveyors to carry out the process. Some even specified that the procedures should be the same as if an Act of Parliament had been obtained.

At the other extreme were the encroachments illegally made upon the common wastes. These were often of very small size, and might involve no more than a neighbouring farmer moving his fence line a few yards into the common, but when carried out over a substantial period of time such gradual attrition might totally eliminate a common.

The distinctions between the different types and methods of enclosure are no mere minor points of academic and legal interest, for their potential impact on farming structure and the rural landscape was very different, and much confusion has arisen through failure to make clear precisely which type of enclosure is being discussed. The enclosure of common fields and of common wastes was, in many ways, not one process but two, even though they were often carried out together in a particular parish or manor. The former was a relatively straightforward process, for the proportion of land due to each individual was obvious from the areas of the strips which they occupied. All that was normally necessary was to divide up the land in the same proportions as those in which they were currently held.

In the simplest case this did not even involve any change of properties: owners merely took sole control of their own strips, with all communal controls over cropping patterns and all common rights ceasing to exist. Such a solution removed restraints which many in the eighteenth and nineteenth centuries felt increasingly irksome, and was widely adopted in Continental Europe, giving rise to the patchwork of tiny strips still visible in parts of France and Germany. In England it was more usual to take the further step of attempting at least some measure of consolidation, and reducing the multitude of small strips into a handful of compact blocks per owner. This produced a landscape of much larger, often rectangular fields, and in terms of farming efficiency offered far greater prospects for large-scale production and for mechanisation. For these reasons, it was much favoured by such advocates of agricultural improvement as Arthur Young and by progressive landowners anxious to increase the productivity of their estates, but it brought with it complications at enclosure. Since it involved exchanging land there were endless opportunities for dispute. It was hardly likely that land quality would be uniform over the thousand acres or so which might represent a large common field system, so giving an owner a 50-acre block in one area in exchange for his 50 acres of scattered strips might be unfair. On the other hand, persuading him that 40 acres of better land was equivalent in value was unlikely to be easy.

Compensation for tithes could be a further complication in attempting such wholesale reorganisation. In theory, tithes were intended to support the local priest, with a contribution towards the upkeep of the wider Church hierarchy, and consisted of a payment of one tenth of the produce from each farm in the community. In practice, the situation had long been more complex. Tithes had been split between the *impropriator* (the 'patron' of the church) and the vicar, and by the eighteenth century ownership of the impropriatorial tithes had frequently passed into the hands of a whole range of landowners and institutions with little connection to the local parish, or even the Church.[1] Payment of tithe in kind was a major irritant to eighteenth century farmers, and enclosure offered an opportunity to get rid of the practice, by offering the tithe owner land in exchange for its abolition. If this were not done, the hoped-for improvements in productivity would merely put still more into the hands of the tithe owner, who would be entitled to one tenth of any increase. However, if the tithe owner were to be compensated in land for the abolition of his rights in kind, this would involve a substantial reduction in the amount available for redistribution amongst the owners. Writers such as Neeson (1993) have made much of the possible damaging effects of this upon the small farmer, but it is easy to exaggerate the impact. Many enclosures did not involve tithe commutation: some parishes had already made arrangements for this prior to enclosure, and in others, tithes continued to be paid in kind on the newly enclosed land. Young points out that, where tithe owners were over-rapacious, their demands were often simply ignored, and enclosures carried out without any attempt to replace payments in kind. His analysis of 74 cases reveals that 42 retained such payments (Young, 1808, p. 36).

Enclosure of the common wastes stands in sharp contrast. The essential aim (if not always the actual result) of such enclosure was to bring to a high level of productivity lands which were underused. It was thus in intent a reclamation movement, rather than one of property consolidation. Furthermore, the problems facing the enclosers were of a very different order, for there was no equivalent to the direct stake in a measurable piece of land which simplified the task of enclosing those fields. In some wastes, stinting was in operation, whereby each owner had rights to turn out specified numbers of animals, but even then it was normal for other individuals to have rights to gather brushwood for fuel, to cut turf or peat and to dig stone or clay for repairs to their properties. Worse still, many wastes, probably the majority nationally, were unstinted, so that there was no measure even of the relative proportions due to individuals for their pasture rights, let alone any other additional ones which they might possess.

The position was further complicated by the question of entitlement to rights. Many communities, though by no means all, adopted a fairly generous attitude towards the landless and allowed them to exercise some rights which, in strict legal terms, they did not possess. When the moment for enclosure came, this could become a major cause of dispute. The desire to exclude outsiders who were misusing rights or squatting on the common was often the trigger which set enclosure in motion but, if the rules were imposed sufficiently rigidly to exclude them, there was a great danger that genuine local users might also lose their entitlement. Proof to the standards which the law would require might be beyond many in a society where illiteracy was still common and where rights had formerly derived from custom and usage, rather than written documents. It was not, of course, that the law ignored custom and usage – it did not – but in a contested enclosure, an individual's claims to rights might be disputed by others. For example, it was often stated in enclosure acts that encroachments on a common should be regarded as the property of the encroachers if they were of more than twenty years' standing, with any of shorter duration being included as part of the common. The memory of witnesses as to whether a particular piece of land had been taken in twenty or twenty-one years before could therefore be of vital importance in determining an individual's ownership.

Two other types of land contributed to the enclosure process, though to a far lesser degree. Common meadow played a vital part in the agriculture of many communities, since the hay cut from it was often the only available supplement to the meagre winter pasture of the commons and the crop-free fields. In terms of area it was normally of no great extent, though locally, for example in the valley of the Hampshire Avon, it could occupy a substantial part of some parishes. The fairness of the division of a common meadow was of considerable significance to those involved, but from the technical point of view this was no different from the enclosure of the common arable. Those concerned normally held known strips, as in the fields, or, in some cases in the southern counties, shares which were converted into specific pieces of meadow by a draw made at regular intervals.

Secondly, there were the *old enclosures* which make a frequent appearance in many enclosure awards. Such lands were, by definition, already enclosed and held in severalty before the agreement was signed or the bill drawn up and were therefore technically in no need of enclosure. However, small detached portions of land were only marginally more useful to the large landowner than strips in the open fields, and enclosure provided an ideal opportunity to reorganise them into more compact blocks at the same time. This could be done either by throwing such plots into the initial pool of land to be enclosed, or by arranging private deals to exchange them for other land, often the new allotments in the former fields or on the former commons. In the first case, these plots are sometimes difficult to distinguish in the award, for the commissioners carrying out the enclosure simply treated them as part of the open land, though of course making an appropriate allowance to the landowner who had relinquished them. In the second, the arrangement was technically just a private arrangement between the two owners, but confirmed by the commissioners as a device to establish their legal validity. However, there is ample evidence that the commissioners were often aware of the proposed deals, and laid out the other allotments with an eye to maximising the efficiency of the new holdings that would result after the exchanges had taken place.

All of these types of land could be enclosed by any of a range of legally distinct methods. The simplest possibility was where the lord of the manor succeeded in obtaining sole possession of all the common land and all the rights in it. If, for example, the common fields of a village lay entirely within one manor, and all the holdings within them were held by tenants of that manor, the lord could simply wait for each tenancy to come to an end. He could thus gradually accumulate all the fields into his own hands and eventually reorganise as he wished. The process could take a great deal of time, especially where tenancies for several lives were involved, and might prove impossible if there were hereditable copyholders, but the process was certainly widely used.

In the case of commons, the same process was possible, though the complications were liable to be greater. Again, if the lord could acquire all the common rights they would simply cease to exist, since there was no longer anyone to exercise them. However, the number and complexity of rights over the same piece of land tended in practice to act as a barrier. A single cottager determined to continue to collect fuel could, in theory, block the way. Nevertheless, there are plenty of examples of lords succeeding in enclosing in this way, such as Duncton, West Sussex, where Lord Leconfield acquired all the rights by 1821 (Leconfield, 1954).

A legally more complex case arose from the fact that a landowner had an implied right to use his land as he wished, providing that in doing so he did not impinge on the rights of others. To what extent this allowed him to remove his land from communal use was a matter of dispute amongst the legal authorities of the time. In the case of the common fields there was, as has already been indicated, a strong body of opinion that they were not, strictly speaking, common at all. In this view, the 'common rights' exercised over the fields were in reality no more than a tacit mutual agreement amongst the proprietors not to enforce the laws of trespass against each other (Gonner, 1912, p. 10). If this view were legally valid, there would be nothing to prevent any proprietor from withdrawing his land from a common field system at any time, providing that he also simultaneously abandoned any claim to grazing rights over the other proprietors' strips.

Other authorities took a different view. The legal niceties of the argument varied, but in essence it was that, since the fields were common by immemorial custom, no individual could unilaterally withdraw from them. The very act of withdrawing land was held to infringe the rights of the other parties, and could thus be legally challenged.

Given this divergence of views, an individual taking unilateral action might get away with it, but it was equally possible that he might face a legal action which he might or might not win. In practice, as will be shown later, this method of enclosure was highly important in the counties under consideration, but it was always a risky business for the proprietor concerned.

In the case of the common pastures and wastes, the position was technically clearer, but in practice equally open to legal squabbling. All such commons had an owner, normally the lord of the manor, and under the Statutes of Westminster (1285) and of Merton (1236) he had a legal right to enclose parts of the common at will, providing that he left sufficient land open to meet the legitimate claims of the owners of common rights. It was this last proviso which was a potential source of problems, since it was difficult to prove that the land left open was indeed adequate for the right-owners. Destructive exploitation, such as peat-cutting rights, created special difficulties, since once the peat had been cut from an area the cutters needed to move on, and if the rest of the land had been enclosed they were unable to do so, thus depriving them of their rights. Grazing rights were theoretically less of a barrier but, if the common was small, restricting the animals to a part of it could easily lead to over-grazing, so enclosure was liable to be vigorously resisted. Again, this method of enclosure was very widely used, but legal wrangles were frequent, as were other forms of resistance, such as the breaking-down of fences.

One obvious way of reducing the possibility of dispute was to arrange an agreement amongst all the parties, preferably one written in proper legal form, which could be relied upon in a court of law. If all the parties concerned with the common fields agreed, there was nothing to stop them from abolishing all communal controls and dealing with their own land as they wished. Better still, the possibility existed of exchanging the existing strips in order to consolidate holdings, so that a more economically rational pattern of farm units could be achieved. The same also applied to the commons, with the obvious proviso that, since none of the right-owners held any specific part of the common, some formal division had to take place. This was clearly a potential sticking point, since even if all parties were in total agreement in principle, this was a rather different matter from agreeing to accept a specific piece of land in compensation for the rights given up. Therefore, there evolved the habit of appointing a panel of individuals, variously known as arbitrators, referees or (later but most frequently) commissioners, to carry out the division of the land on the proprietors' behalf. Written into the agreement was a clause stating that all parties agreed to accept the arbitrators' award. Indeed, in some later agreements, it was specifically stated that the procedures and the powers of the commissioners should be the same as if an Act of Parliament had been obtained. The Bashley (Hampshire) agreement of 1815, for example, used precisely this phraseology.[2]

One of the most significant barriers to the wider use of formal agreements was the existence of legal doubts over the right of many owners to bind their successors in title. Much of the land in southern England was actually in the hands, not of a single individual, but of various types of institution, such as the colleges of Oxford and Cambridge Universities, Winchester College, or a multitude of charities, large and small. It was at the very least arguable that the officials acting for these institutions had no powers to alienate land or rights, even in exchange for equivalent land or rights elsewhere. At Longstock (Hampshire) the bursar of Corpus Christi College, Oxford, agonised for a long time over whether he could sign an agreement, and was eventually persuaded only by the news that the authorities at Magdalen College were quite happy to do so.[3]

By far the biggest of these institutional landowners (apart from the Crown) was the Church in its various guises, and Church lands rights posed a major problem. The Deans and Chapters, notably of Winchester, were the nominal owners of huge areas of land, and found themselves in much the same position as the bursar of Corpus Christi. Could the Dean sign an agreement which would bind his successors for ever, especially if the land concerned had been granted to the Church on condition that it was to be inalienable? Some took the risk, working on the theory that the advantages of enclosure were such that no-one would be likely to challenge their decision, but many must have felt that they might suffer personal actions for exceeding their powers. In any case, the other owners involved faced the possibility that if they concluded an agreement their subsequent improvements might be thrown into jeopardy by some future Dean.

A similar, and often more serious, problem was the existence of *glebe land*.[4] The incumbent was in effect a tenant for life, and any agreement which he entered into could almost certainly be challenged by his successors should they wish. Not every parish had glebe land, and not all the glebe land was in the open fields, or possessed common rights, but a very high proportion of those parishes wishing to enclose were likely to face the problem. The problem was not insurmountable, especially if the gift of the living was in the hands of a patron, who could put pressure on any future holder of the post, but once again it introduced an element of uncertainty.

Finally, it must be remembered that much family estate land passed through periods when it was in the hands of trustees or guardians, whose freedom of action was often severely restricted. Minors were unable to take charge of their estates until they reached the age of majority, and many families in the eighteenth and nineteenth centuries used settlements to ensure that the family lands could not be lost or squandered, even when they did. This particularly affected land passed on to daughters, since there was always a danger that the husband might divert the land from the direct line of descent if, for example, the wife died and he remarried. He might then pass the land to the children of the second marriage, in preference to those of the first. Putting the land in trust, so that only the revenues could be spent but the land itself could not be alienated, ensured that this could not happen. It also ensured, however, that the tenant for life could not sign a valid agreement to dispose of this land, even in exchange for other lands regarded as of equal value.

One obvious way out of the dilemma was to use the power of Parliament. Parliament had long been accustomed to the idea of an individual or group of individuals using an act as a means of overcoming purely personal or local problems which could not be dealt with within the law as it existed at the time, such as naturalisation or divorce. The use of such a procedure to effect an enclosure was in no way unprecedented. Indeed, the earliest enclosure acts arise so naturally from what had gone before that there is some scope for argument about whether they should really be regarded as enclosures at all. As has already been suggested, perhaps Ropley (Hampshire) rather than Radipole (Dorset) has the best claim to be the first true enclosure.

Early enclosure acts were often used merely to ensure the legality of an agreement already drawn up, and even already put into effect. They were thus not necessarily followed by an award detailing the new allocation of the land, as was usually the case. A few acts even contain the details of the award within them, though it was more normal simply to confirm the pre-existing arrangements without specifying them in detail. There were also occasional examples where there was only a single owner, who presumably felt the need to obtain an act to ensure that there was no possibility of a later challenge. The East Wellow (Hampshire) Act, for example, empowered the Duke of Chandos to enclose East Wellow Common, while that for Odiham (in the same county) did the same for Pawlet St John in respect of Hillside Common, specifying that St John had reached an agreement with all other potential claimants and that this agreement was to be legally valid. However, such confirmatory acts are relatively few as a proportion of the total, only 12 out of 535 in the counties under consideration in this book, and they are largely confined to the period before 1770, though there were occasional examples at a much later date.[5] Most enclosure acts, however, were drawn up prior to the enclosure, in order to give the necessary authority to proceed. They could thus be used, and indeed were used, to over-ride opposition by some of the parties involved, though the existence of an act cannot necessarily be taken, as it sometimes is, as evidence of resistance.

Motivation

Given this great variation in the enclosure process, it is hardly surprising that no single explanation of the motivation and driving mechanisms behind it holds good for all cases. A number of general explanations have been offered, but these are not necessarily applicable to all places at all times. Turner, for example, offers the suggestion that parliamentary enclosure owed much of its impetus to the lack of pasture land, and hence the need to enable common arable to be laid down to grass (Turner, 1980, p 150-1). While this was undoubtedly valid in parts of the Midlands in the mid-eighteenth century, it was hardly applicable to the counties under consideration here, where there was generally abundant grazing land. The majority of the land enclosed was, in any case, common pasture, not common arable, and there is ample evidence that far from arable being converted to pasture, in many areas new open fields were being created from downland. Similarly, the suggestion that the whole process was a plot by large landowners to deprive the small ones of their land and rights (for example, Thompson, 1966, p. 218) is, at best, a gross oversimplification. Many landowners had ample opportunity to remove copyholders and tenants without recourse to enclosure, had that been their primary aim. The evidence in a number of cases is that the situation was reversed: it was the desire to enclose that led landowners to remove tenants in order to simplify the process. Furthermore, there are many instances of the tenants urging landlords to enclose.

The fundamental underlying motive for enclosure was simply to make agriculture more efficient. There was a general belief, widely though not universally held at the time, that enclosed land was more productive than land which was common, and that enclosure would therefore allow productivity to be significantly increased. In the words of Arthur Young, one of the principal protagonists of enclosure, 'An Act of Enclosure frees the cultivator from the shackles in which he was before manacled' (Young, 1808, p. 44). From the national point of view, this meant that the amount of food being produced would rise, thus helping to stave off the disaster which Malthus and others predicted, namely that the rising population would outstrip the ability of agriculture to feed them. From the point of view of the landowner, greater productivity would lead to a higher income, either directly through a greater surplus to sell, or indirectly through higher rents chargeable to tenants anxious to obtain the more productive land.

Some modern writers have argued that open field land, specifically, was not necessarily less productive than its enclosed equivalent (for example, Allen, 1982, p. 948), but this is not relevant to the point under discussion here. What is significant is that most contemporaries *believed* that it was, and it was this which governed their actions. Moreover, the argument scarcely applies to the common wastes, which formed the greater part of the land enclosed. Few of these could possibly have been agriculturally more productive in their open than in their enclosed state. Occasionally they were so badly mishandled after enclosure that financial and environmental disaster followed but, in general, the mere fact that they were individually owned opened the way to a more rational and balanced pattern of management, even if nothing were done to alter the nature of the vegetation or soil.

At the local level, where decisions about whether or not to enclose were actually made, a range of other considerations came into play. There is much evidence to suggest that it was not so much the positive merits of enclosure as the negative aspects of the existing system which finally pushed local communities to act. Foremost of these was the potential misuse of grazing rights, to the detriment of the local farmer. The rules governing grazing rights varied enormously, even between neighbouring parishes or manors, but most were open to abuse in one way or another. Many manors had a custom that only animals *'levant and couchant'*[6] on a holding could make use of pasture rights but, since the buying and selling of stock was a normal part of a farming enterprise, some element of flexibility was essential if the system was to work in practice. This obviously left a loophole for individuals to operate a judiciously timed programme of buying and selling which would allow them to keep more animals on the common than they could possibly sustain on their other lands.

Stinting was another means by which over-exploitation of the resources of the commons was traditionally kept in check and, providing the rules were strictly enforced, this normally worked well. However, ensuring that the rules were adhered to was an expensive and time-consuming job, especially where the commons were extensive, and many stewards neglected this aspect of their duties. At Horsham (Sussex), Charles Medwin, steward to the Duke of Norfolk, made little attempt to prevent abuses until forced to act by the protests of the various right-owners. Ironically, several of the protesters were amongst those brought to court when he did eventually act (Chapman, 1982, pp. 185-191).

The situation was potentially far worse where no stinting arrangements existed. In many manors the prospects of the commons ever being over-stocked must have seemed extremely remote in the Middle Ages, when the rules were crystallising. In what were essentially subsistence communities, individuals would not have had the resources to buy in significant numbers of stock, and there would normally have been little incentive for outsiders to become involved, unless the manor happened to be close to a major market. In many cases, therefore, stints must have seemed quite unnecessary, and were certainly never laid down.

In the changed circumstances of the eighteenth and nineteenth centuries, unstinted commons offered a tempting target for anyone seeking to make a quick profit. With a rising population, and more especially a rising urban and industrial population, the potential for commercial agriculture was greatly expanded, and as industry appeared in new areas, previously remote farming communities found a new market on their doorsteps. Any farmer, smallholder or even cottager able to lay hands on a large number of stock could turn as many as he wished on the unstinted commons. The fact that these animals might devastate the common, leaving little or nothing for stock to eat in succeeding months, was of little significance to him if the animals were to be sold on; for the small-scale farmer attempting to maintain a balanced system, and reliant on the common for pasture throughout the whole permitted season, this could be a disaster.

Obviously, under normal circumstances, few (if any) local farmers could afford to buy sufficient stock to bring about problems on any scale, but there were opportunities for outsiders with much greater financial resources to become involved. Graziers and butchers could often bribe a cottager or smallholder to pass off stock as his own, and thus find cheap pasture for large numbers of animals. This was of course illegal, but unless the manorial officials were exceptionally alert and active, it was likely to be too late by the time that the case was brought before the court. The damage would already have been done. There was also a perfectly good legal alternative open to the outsiders, namely to buy rights for themselves. The cheapest way of doing this varied according to local custom, but it was often to buy a cottage with rights attached; the cottage could then be let, and unlimited use made of the common. A small piece of land might serve just as well in some manors.

A further threat from outside came from drovers. Large numbers of stock were driven long distances to urban markets, or to fattening grounds far from the rearing areas in the higher lands of the north and west of the country. Any village on the line of these movements faced the prospect of playing temporary host to these flocks and herds, again with potentially disastrous results to their commons. Once more, the damage was likely to have been done, and the drovers long gone, before formal legal action could be taken.

The role of poor squatters as an irritant was probably relatively localised. Only where commons were small and squatters numerous was it likely to become a serious problem, though as commons in any area began to be enclosed, the problem tended to be pushed onto those remaining open. Squatters, however, not only took land for their dwellings but, once settled, usually attempted to make use of the commons, even though they technically had no right to do so. Indeed, it would have been extremely difficult for them to have survived in many areas without at the very least gathering firewood or other fuel from the common. There was also a temptation for them to attempt to run animals on the common. This is often pictured as a cow, but in reality, it is unlikely that many squatters would have had the finance to purchase one, nor would they have had the resources to keep it during the season when animals would have had to be removed from the common. More realistically, they would have been likely to keep a few poultry or a pig. However, by using the resources of the commons, they came into direct competition with those who were legally entitled to rights, and there was an incentive for locals to attempt to stop them.

Other factors added to the pressure on the commons. The right to dig stone, gravel or sand was frequently allowed by local custom, and was again open to abuse as conditions changed. Growing towns demanded large quantities of building materials, and nearby commons often provided the builder with a cheap and convenient source. Portsmouth Common became pitted with holes, which not merely deprived the stock of grazing land but presented a physical danger to them.[7]

The most certain way of stopping these problems was to enclose the land concerned and physically fence out the intruders, and there is ample evidence that it was factors such as these which finally persuaded some local populations that enclosure was essential. In these circumstances, it was not necessarily the lord of the manor who had the greatest incentive to act. Indeed, since he was in a position to extract rent from squatters, he may even have had something to gain by allowing the misuse to continue, especially if he himself was not involved in depasturing animals. On the other hand, for the farmer on the edge of viability, a diminution in the value of his rights could finally tip the balance against him, and he might well feel that enclosure was the lesser of the two evils. At Horsham (Sussex), as has already been discussed, enclosure, far from being actively pursued by the lord, was a reluctant response to years of complaints from the local community. Similarly, at Amberley (Sussex) local farmers and landowners were frustrated for some nine years in their efforts to obtain an act by the indifference of the lord of the manor, Lord Selsey,[8] and the whole business dragged on for 28 years before the final award was completed. The traditional picture of the lord and one or two major landowners enthusiastically pushing through enclosure as a means of grabbing more land, against the opposition of the local small farmers, is thus far from universally applicable.

The Procedures

The procedures necessary to achieve enclosure obviously varied greatly with the method chosen, which in turn was determined largely by specific local conditions, though prevailing fashion seems to have played some part.

In theory, the simplest method was unity of possession, but in practice this proved the most difficult to achieve in the area and period under consideration. Though it occasionally proved possible, as at Warnford (Hampshire) and Throope (Wiltshire), in the overwhelming majority of cases the lord of the manor was faced with other freeholders or right owners, and was obliged to seek alternative methods. This is not to imply that central-southern England was a land of owner-occupying yeoman farmers in 1700. Frequently, the other freeholders were few in number, and were often themselves letting their land to tenant farmers, but the existence of a even a single freeholder was sufficient to deny the lord the unity essential for this means of enclosure. The ultimate barrier was often the existence of glebe land, for whereas other owners might be persuaded to sell, the parson was legally incapable of disposing of the glebe.

Where the lord did succeed in acquiring all lands and rights, he could simply wait for all tenancies to fall vacant, though this might take a considerable period of time. The ideal situation from the lord's point of view was one where the land was let to tenants at will or on one-year leases, but this was unusual. In the eighteenth century, land was often let for a number of lives, usually three, which made it impossible to predict when the land would revert and, when leases for a specific term became more common, 21 years was frequently chosen, thus imposing a lengthy period before consolidation could occur.

Copyholds presented similar problems. Again, they were widespread in 1700, and though they tended to decrease in numbers with time, they were still by no means unusual in 1852, when measures for their gradual abolition were introduced by Parliament.[9] Like leases, they came in various forms, one of the commonest again being for three lives. At the other extreme were the hereditable copyholds which had no fixed term, and could be handed down from generation to generation, which effectively prevented them ever reverting to the lord unless the line died out, or some individual defaulted on the customary payments.

In these circumstances, it was in the lord's interest (if he were the motivating force behind the enclosure) to attempt to quicken the process. Buying out the lease or the copyholder was one obvious way, and large landowners with extensive estates could often find an alternative farm on favourable terms to encourage the tenant to move. The mere offer of an enclosed farm of equal size may have seemed worthwhile to many, and if the lord was prepared to offer, for example, to add an extra life to a copyhold, that might remove any remaining objections. No doubt a combination of a favourable offer, and suggestions that things could be made awkward if it were rejected, were used on occasions to move a reluctant individual.

For the small landowner or copyholder who wished to enclose open field land, the easiest and cheapest method was to simply to fence off his holding and withdraw it from the system. As has already been indicated, there was a body of opinion which held that he had a perfect right to do so and, if he were to be challenged, this would have to be in the manorial courts, which tended to become less and less effective as the eighteenth century wore on. By the end of the century many courts were completely moribund, so a determined encloser had little prospect of being overthrown.

In practice, there is no reason to presume that anyone would necessarily wish to overthrow it. Piecemeal enclosure of open fields was able to occur on such a large scale precisely because it was rarely in the interests of any of the parties to oppose it. It imposed no costs on the small farmer, such as parliamentary enclosure did, since he was under no obligation to fence his own land merely because a neighbour had. The tithe owner had nothing to lose, since he was still collecting the same tithes from the same land, and even if the land were copyhold or leasehold, the lord or landowner normally had no reason to object, unless he felt that it might interfere with plans of his own for a wholesale reorganisation of the area.

Evidence from the central southern counties, and indeed elsewhere, suggests that a variant on these two related processes was often by far the most important, and that was 'unity of possession' at the tenant level. The assumption that tenants were inevitably small farmers creeps into many discussions of eighteenth-and nineteenth-century agrarian matters, but this was not necessarily so. Many were farmers on a substantial scale, and by a careful policy of leasing or renting from a variety of different owners, they were often able to bring whole furlongs, whole fields, or even occasionally whole systems under their control. Once both land and grazing rights were in their hands, the fact that there were several owners became irrelevant, since both common rotations and grazing rights effectively ceased to exist. Legally they still remained, since if one owner terminated the arrangement he could reinstate them, but in practice there can have been little incentive to do so.

Enclosing the common piecemeal was legally a different matter, for there was no assumed right to any particular portion of the common, and anyone other than the lord who fenced off a piece was encroaching. Even the lord's rights to enclose under the Statutes of Westminster and Merton were open to dispute, since the onus was on him to prove that he had left sufficient to satisfy the legal rights of the other owners. In practice, encroachments were very frequent, and unless the local steward was particularly active and determined, the encroacher was liable to succeed. Even if the court imposed fines, these were often so small as to be little deterrent, and many met so infrequently that action could take a very long period of time. The Horsham court, referred to earlier, was apparently not held between 1742 and 1787. An encroacher who held on for 21 years without being forced to pay rent, or being otherwise formally obliged to acknowledge any other authority over the land, established a presumed ownership to it which was very difficult to overthrow.

Again, there is no necessity to assume that the process would be opposed. If the lord could extract rent, he might well be only too pleased to see 'unproductive' land reclaimed. Indeed, lords regularly granted licences to take in portions of the common. Those most likely to object were, in fact, the other small farmers or smallholders, since every encroachment reduced the acreage available for the exercise of their own common rights. If, as was often the case, they themselves were encroaching, complaints were likely to be muted.

The principal problem with piecemeal enclosure was that it left the fragmented ownership pattern of the open fields unchanged, and that piecemeal enclosure of the commons, if anything, tended to increase it. Private bilateral arrangements might allow some consolidation, but unless there were only two or three owners, some formal agreement was normally necessary.

As has been mentioned, such agreements might take a wide variety of forms, and the processes needed to achieve them varied in consequence. At the simplest level, they might involve no more than a formalisation of a piecemeal enclosure, with all parties agreeing to fence the lands which they already occupied and to forego any communal rights, as at Ludgershall (Wiltshire).[10] This, however, though offering some measure of legal protection in the event of a later dispute, failed to deal with the fundamental problem of fragmentation, and such agreements are rare.

More usually, the agreement was to accept reorganised holdings in the place of the old, which must have seemed a far more drastic step to some of those concerned. It must normally have involved someone being deputed to lay out the new holdings though in relatively simple cases, with few landowners, it may have been possible to achieve the desired result by a simple process of exchanges. However, it often proved easier to obtain agreement on the principle of enclosure than on the detail of how it should be done, and the commonest form was one whereby the parties bound themselves to accept the arbitration of a group of named individuals, who would lay out a new pattern of holdings.

It would be naive to assume that such agreements were greeted with equal enthusiasm by all, or that threats were not used from time to time to break down the resistance of a few recalcitrant individuals. The few surviving private papers dealing with the process give ample indication of the wrangling which went on, and the types of pressure which were occasionally used to produce the necessary 'unanimity'. Threats not to renew tenancies or extend copyholds could be very effective if the time remaining until expiry was very short. Even more effective, in the later eighteenth and nineteenth centuries, was the threat of an enclosure act, since in that case the objector would almost certainly lose, and would be subject to far greater expenses into the bargain. Why waste time and money fighting the inevitable?

The procedures for obtaining an enclosure act were the most complex, the most long-winded, and the most expensive, and it was thus a last resort. However, it did have the advantage of legal certainty, for if one were obtained the only effective challenge was if fraud or legal errors could be proved.

An enclosure act followed precisely the same parliamentary process as any other private act, and a detailed account is contained in Turner (1978, pp. 23-28). Briefly, a petition was presented to Parliament asking leave to bring in a bill, and this was normally ordered to be done. Only if the proposal was in breach of standing orders (or was faced with powerful opposition) was leave refused, and the petition referred to a committee, who had to be satisfied before the bill could proceed. The bill was presented and read twice, then referred to a committee with responsibility for hearing any counter-petitions and for investigating the accuracy of, for example, the alleged support for the bill. Amendments were sometimes ordered at this stage. The bill was then reported to the full house, read a third time and sent to the Lords, after which, assuming it was passed without amendment, it received the royal assent.

In practice, from the point of view of the promoters, much of the work had been completed before these formal stages were reached. Even for a parliamentary enclosure, a substantial measure of agreement was necessary for a bill to stand any chance of success, and reaching such an agreement might be extremely time-consuming. Most parliamentary enclosures no doubt started through casual conversations between proprietors and their agents, and these early stages are inevitably difficult to trace. It seems highly probable that in a substantial proportion of cases, it was only when the possibilities of enclosing by agreement had been exhausted that the idea of presenting a bill came to the fore.

The first task was to determine that there was, indeed, sufficient support for the proposed bill. Parliament was not always consistent in interpreting the rules, and these changed from time to time (Turner, 1978, p. 27), but support from the owners of two-thirds of the land or rights was always required, and three-quarters or four-fifths was normally demanded. One or two dominant owners might meet this requirement on their own, but in the majority of cases more were needed. In the ten per cent sample of the central southern counties, almost 54 per cent of enclosures needed the consent of at least three owners to meet even the two-thirds rule, and at Framfield (Sussex) 15 were required. Where proprietors were numerous, the promoters often found it necessary to call a public meeting to try to gauge the strength of support, but this must have been a last resort since it served to alert any opposition to what was proposed. There were obvious advantages in giving opponents as little time as possible to mount a counter campaign, and in a letter preserved with the Fordington (Dorset) enclosure papers Thomas Davis, the well-known enclosure commissioner, specifically suggests that the bill be passed round in private, rather than having a public meeting where opponents will gather and friends will be less willing to speak out.[11] Parliament eventually stepped in to insist that proposals to present a bill must be advertised on the doors of the relevant parish churches for three successive Sundays, following a number of complaints that interested parties were unaware of a bill's existence.

The methods by which the promoters sought to persuade, cajole or bully reluctant proprietors into supporting them are only rarely recorded, and the extent of the pressure can only be guessed at. It must be stressed, however, that the picture often presented of one or two powerful landowners cowing the opposition of hosts of powerless small proprietors by threats, is largely an exaggeration. The initiative did not always come from the large proprietors, nor were they always unanimously in favour, any more than the smaller were unanimously against. In the Fordington case just mentioned, Davis specifically identifies 'certain attorneys in Dorchester' as opponents, and the implication of his letter is that supporters were unwilling to be publicly identified, suggesting that the pressure was not all on one side. Similarly, at the Broyle enclosure in Ringmer (Sussex) the opposition was led by William Kemp(e), a major local landowner and a Sargeant at Law, who organised a counter-petition to Parliament,[12] (Kay, 1979). In reality, there were often few small proprietors left, either to oppose or support the proposals. In almost 28 per cent of the sample parliamentary enclosures, the number of individuals involved, including the tithe owner, was in single figures, and many of the 'small proprietors' were, in fact, men of substance. It was usually only in the large waste enclosures that large numbers of genuine small owner-occupiers and cottagers appear.

Counter-petitions to Parliament were not infrequent, though it is difficult to gauge their success. Merely looking at those bills which progressed some way through the parliamentary procedures gives the impression that such petitions were usually ignored, since a large number of the acts were passed in spite of them. It would appear that at least 34 of the 535 individual acts in the area faced such opposition. However, Turner's evidence is that nationally, some thousand bills failed to become law, which is approximately 1 in 6. It is also likely that, in most cases, a bill facing serious opposition was simply withdrawn or not proceeded with at an early stage, when the promoters realised that their chances of success were small.[13] Opposition may thus have been rather more successful than at first appears, especially when account is taken of the number of attempts which did not even reach the stage of drawing up an initial bill.

Once a bill had become law, the commissioners officially began their work on dividing and redistributing the land. They needed to familiarise themselves with the land concerned, if they had not already done so, to arrange for it to be surveyed, either by one of their number or by an appointed specialist, and to determine who was entitled to a share in the allocation. This last was one of the most sensitive parts of their work, since it involved them in adjudicating on disputes, and their decision was hardly likely to please the loser. The procedure was to call for all concerned to submit claims, which were then open to general inspection. Objections could then be made by any of the other parties to any of the claims, in which case the commissioners called for evidence from the claimant. This point is of some significance, since the Hammonds and others have made much of the fact that many small owners would be unable to produce legally satisfactory evidence of their claims, and were liable to lose out as a result (Hammond, J.L. and B., 1911). In practice, they were often not required to do so, since objections to individual small claims were not common. In the case of small farmers with land in open fields or meadows, objections were highly unlikely, since possession of the existing holding was normally adequate proof in itself. Occasional disputes arose over claims by neighbours that an individual had encroached on an adjoining strip, for example at Odiham (Hampshire), where a tenant of Sir Henry Paulet St John was alleged to have ploughed up a boundary baulk owned by Corpus Christi College,[14] and there were sometimes disputes over whether land was, for example, freehold or leasehold, as at Chesilbourne (Dorset), but these were of no general significance.

Claims to rights over the common were more contentious, but again the evidence is that most were never opposed. At the Broyle for example, smallholders were only required to prove usage, which could be readily done from the evidence of their neighbours. The most common objections in such situations were on manorial or territorial grounds, in which case the smallholders were not left to fight the case on their own, but became mere bystanders in a battle between the lords of the manors. At the Broyle, Henry Burtenshaw and William Kemp attempted to show that rights were restricted to Ringmer manor, which brought them into conflict with the Bishop of Durham and others with land in Glynde and Stoneham, a battle which they eventually lost when the Bishop produced grants to rights on the waste.

The commissioners frequently took oral evidence from the oldest residents when disputes did occur, and relied heavily on them, particularly when the point at issue was the length of time over which rights had been exercised. Robert Fisher Gills for example, commissioner for the Beeston and Pitcroft enclosure in Portsmouth, accepted the evidence of Robert Moses, aged 70, against the claims of the Borough of Portsmouth. A modern search of the documentary evidence reveals that the Borough had a case, but the fact that rights had not been exercised in living memory was sufficient to convince Gills that he should reject the claims.[15]

Again, following the Hammonds, it is often assumed that there was no appeal against the commissioners' decisions, but this is not so. Most acts make specific arrangements for appeals, normally to the Quarter Sessions, though in Somerset and Durham arbitrators were often appointed. Such appeals procedures were used. John Upperton successfully disputed the commissioners' judgement at the Thakeham, Sullington and Shipley (Sussex) enclosure, and he was by no means unique.[16] Clearly, such a course of action was only available to those with some financial resources and, even amongst the wealthy, there was often a feeling that there was little point in bothering to challenge the allotment. Upperton, though successful, did not receive any land, since by the time the case had been heard the new owners had already taken possession of their allotments and attempting to redraw the boundaries at that stage would have caused enormous disruption. Whether he regarded the monetary payment in lieu as adequate compensation is not recorded.

Once the claims had been determined, the reorganisation of the land could begin. This frequently involved 'old enclosures', i.e. land that was already in individual occupation, since the incorporation of these allowed a much more efficient layout of the resulting holdings. It was common practice to include a clause in the act that detached fields of under three acres should be reallocated, and land with more than one owner within a single ring fence was often included as well. More important was the provision for owners to voluntarily throw enclosed land into the pool, or for the commissioners to confirm exchanges of old enclosed land as part of their award. The landowners surrendering land, whether compulsorily or voluntarily, obviously received appropriate recompense at the allotment. From the point of view of the landowners, this not only allowed them to dispose of small, isolated (and in some cases almost useless land) in exchange for solid blocks, but it also gave the force of law to any private deals being carried out. The latter was particularly helpful for those who, as mentioned earlier, had doubts about their legal ability to enter into binding agreements.

There is ample evidence that the commissioners attempted to take account of the wishes of individual landowners in the reallocation process. Numerous letters survive from individuals asking if allotments could be attached to an existing farm or plot of land, or could be laid out in a particular area. For example, eleven letters of this sort exist for the Basing (Hampshire) enclosure. That on behalf of Mrs Booth requesting that her allotment be on the east side of West Field north of the turnpike, or in Home Field, is typical, as is that from Mr Charles Heath, asking that his own allotments and that for his brother's copyhold should be contiguous to each other in either Dean Field or Home Field [17]. Obviously, not all such requests could be met, but there is no evidence that the larger landowners necessarily got preference in this matter. Indeed, it was often easier to satisfy the smaller claimant than to fit the much larger holdings into the preferred area. There is even evidence of commissioners asking the advice of the landowners regarding the precise layout of the new roads. [18]

The fact that commissioners did respond to individual preferences may partly explain the continued fragmentation of holdings after the enclosure process. It was quite normal for even the smaller landholders to receive their new land in several blocks, rather than the single one which might appear to be the optimum solution. However, it has been argued that some owners may have seen merit in maintaining a degree of scatter as a risk-avoidance strategy. [19] On the other hand, it has been suggested that an alternative explanation is that the commissioners not infrequently backed away from the ultimate logic of what they were doing (Chapman, 1992, pp. 181-189). The whole question of valuing the land was contentious enough without deliberately introducing extra points of conflict, and giving one owner all former field land and another all former common or meadow opened up great possibilities for dispute. Giving each a share of each type of land was a way of reducing these, at the expense of perpetuating an element of fragmentation.

One of the problems with such a major property reorganisation was that it usually required a similar reorganisation of roads and watercourses. It was unlikely that the existing roads and rights of way would be appropriate for access to the new holdings, or that the existing watercourses would be so placed that the land could be properly drained. Again, responsibility for creating new patterns fell upon the commissioners. The acts normally gave them full powers to stop up any road or path other than a turnpike, and to create such new ones as were deemed necessary. The same held good for waterways.

The long delays which could occur between act and award would have been disastrous to the whole agricultural system of an area if provision had not been made for cultivation to continue in the interim, and responsibility for overseeing the course of husbandry during this period also fell upon the commissioners. However, they were often able to let the new owners onto their allotments long before the formalities were completed. At Basing, a letter of 8 October 1796 from William Bishop to the Right Hon. Thomas Orde Powlett records that 'Mr Barnes' (George Barnes, one of the commissioners)

> has so far satisfied many of the proprietors as to the situation of their allotments as to enable them to commence a form of husbandry, and others may be referred to us for the same purpose,

though the award was not signed until 23 March 1797.[20]

From the point of view of the modern environment and landscape, one of the most significant powers exercised by the commissioners was that of determining not merely where the new property boundaries should lie, but what they should consist of and the way in which they should be maintained. It was perfectly possible for them to leave the time and method of fencing to the discretion of the owners and this was occasionally done (Chapman, 1976), but this was generally regarded as 'but a half measure',[21] and not to be recommended except in special circumstances. As a consequence, almost all commissioners wrote into their awards quite detailed regulations about the form of boundary to be used and the date by which they should be completed. Even more significantly, either the act or the award normally specified that these boundaries should then be preserved in the prescribed form in perpetuity. With very few exceptions, the form favoured was a quickset hedge. The commissioners were thus responsible for the creation of hedged landscapes over a wide area of England and, at least theoretically, providing a legal protection for them long before the recent legislation.

3

Sources

One of the major problems facing anyone attempting to trace the pattern of enclosure in any area is the lack of a single source of information. The very varied nature of the process itself has left an equally varied documentation, some of it far more obvious and accessible than the rest. Indeed, many of the common misunderstandings and misinterpretations about the movement derive directly from the ready availability, or otherwise, of the records. At one extreme, almost all parliamentary enclosures have left clear documentation of either the beginning or end of the process, if not both; at the other, many informal enclosures have left nothing. In the latter case, careful sifting through a wide range of sources may establish that land was once open or common, and that at some later time it was not, but precisely how or when the change took place may not emerge. Such enclosures are easily overlooked, and this has contributed to the overemphasis on parliamentary enclosure so often found in works on the eighteenth and nineteenth centuries.

This chapter aims to examine the ways in which the enclosure process may be traced, and to look at the advantages and disadvantages of the major sources. Inevitably, it can be only a general guide, for each individual case has its own peculiarities: even the standardised parliamentary awards of the later nineteenth century occasionally deviate from the norm. However, it is hoped that it will serve to guide those seeking to investigate any particular enclosure history, and especially to warn of some of the pitfalls.

For convenience, the various types of enclosure are considered separately, but there is an element of overlap. As will be discussed later, some of the comments about parliamentary awards and maps differ hardly at all from those associated with some formal agreements. Equally, the methods and sources needed to trace informal enclosures have often to be used to pin down formal agreements where the agreements themselves have subsequently been lost. Nevertheless, the means of tracing an enclosure tend to be similar for similar types, so their separation into discrete sections seems appropriate.

Parliamentary Enclosures

The Acts

By definition, every parliamentary enclosure had to have an Act of Parliament as its ultimate authority, and the great majority began formally with an individual act setting out the details of the land to be enclosed and ended with an award specifying how that land had been distributed. However, the General Enclosure Acts of 1836 and 1845, but not that of 1801,[1] removed the need for individual acts,[2] so enclosures under this legislation have left no such record. Subsequent legislation complicated matters still further, for changes to the 1845 act in 1852 meant that later enclosures left behind an 'Order' as their authority, and that their existence is recorded in various consolidated acts put to Parliament by the Enclosure Commission. However, the 1836 act was technically unaffected by this and remained in force until 1899. As a result, occasional enclosures continued to occur without either act or order, quoting the 1836 act as their authority, for example the Hazelbury Bryan (Dorset) enclosure of 1858 or that for Wylie (Wiltshire) in 1861. This legislation was widely used in the central southern counties, especially Dorset, so acts are not infrequently lacking in the area under consideration. Forty-one in the four counties were carried out under the 1836 act alone.

Where an individual act exists, it may not be quite as informative as one might hope. Obviously, all acts had to specify the land to be enclosed, but this might be expressed in very vague terms. 'Certain open and common lands in the parish of..', or some minor variant, is not unusual. For example, the Act 53 George III cap. xxxi is described as 'An Act for inclosing lands in the Parish of Melksham in the County of Wiltshire'. Legal caution also frequently prevailed. It was better to include every possibility amongst the list, since if no land of the specified type existed, no harm was done, whereas if land were accidentally omitted there would be no power to deal with it. The wording of the act is therefore not always a helpful and reliable indication of what was there before enclosure. Ellis (1971, p. 20) records that Tate's method of dividing enclosures into those which contained open field and those which did not, according to the wording of the acts, gives an error rate of one in nine for Wiltshire.

Many acts contain an acreage figure which is stated to be the area involved, but it is often by no means clear what this figure was intended to represent, for it could have covered all the land affected by the enclosure, or merely that which was open or common at the time. Logically, one might expect it to refer to the latter, but in many cases it approximates more closely to the former (Chapman and Harris, 1982). More seriously, it may not approximate very closely to either. After all, much of the land had not been accurately surveyed in the eighteenth and early nineteenth centuries, and indeed it was frequently only enclosure itself which caused this to be done. Those framing the act therefore had to rely on whatever mixture of customary measure and informed guesswork was to hand. The act for Southsea Common (Hampshire) specifically states that it contained 300 *customary* acres, with a further 300 customary acres of morasses and beaches, but many are less precise. The result was that the estimates could be wildly divergent from reality. For example, in the case of Eartham (Sussex), the discrepancy is almost 27 per cent.[3] Even allowing for the fact that the estimate probably included the land allocated for roads, there is still a significant overstatement. Only very rarely indeed do acts specify the acreages of the individual fields or commons to be enclosed, and it is normally impossible to tell from them how much land of each type is involved.

Other information in the acts is equally variable. It was normal practice to name the lord of the manor and some of the principal landowners concerned, but it was very rare to name all of them unless there were only a handful, and social status often took precedence over magnitude of ownership. A major aristocratic landowner was liable to appear, even if he owned only a tiny minority of the land, in preference to a large local landowner of no national social standing. The logic of this for the promoters of the bill is obvious, for the former would be known in Parliament, even if they did not personally have a seat in either House, and their naming in the bill would be liable to ease its passage.

The lord of the manor, as the nominal owner of the soil of any commons, had a particular significance, and arrangements for compensation for his rights normally figure prominently. In particular, the question of whether or not he was relinquishing his mineral rights needed to be established, since this was a potential source of future conflict. If he chose to retain them, then there was a need for clauses to cover the arrangements for access in the event of the lord wishing to exploit them, since he would almost inevitably have to enter someone else's land in order to do so.

Where the tithe situation was to be altered by the enclosure, details of this are invariably included. The consent of the tithe owners to the terms was one of the issues considered by Parliament before they would accept a bill, and there was therefore a need to specify clearly who had a right to the tithe and what arrangements were to be made for their replacement. The percentage of the land to be given in compensation needed to be laid down and it needed to be made clear if, as was normal, the charges of fencing the tithe allotments were to be borne by the other owners. Occasionally, additional clauses were inserted, such as the right of landowners to opt out of the land-for-tithes arrangement and to continue paying in kind, as before.

Arrangements for assuring the fair distribution of the land concerned were crucial to the whole process, and unless the act was merely to confirm an existing agreement, it was normal practice to include the names of the commissioners who would carry it out, together with the process by which they could be replaced if need be. Parliament insisted on this information being present for later acts and refused to accept bills where they were not named, as at Basildon, (Berkshire),[4] reflecting increasing concerns about the impartiality of some commissioners. However, it cannot necessarily be assumed that the individual or individuals named actually carried out the process. Inevitably, some who had initially agreed to be appointed later found themselves unable to take on the task due to illness or pressure of other work, and a significant number died between the passing of the act and the completion of the award. Care is also needed when using copies of the bill (the copies normally found in record offices, and in the British Library collection) rather than the act itself, for Parliament occasionally insisted on changes. At Horsham, for example, a commissioner was replaced at the committee stage in the Commons, though unfortunately no reason for this is recorded.[5]

The surveyor responsible for measuring the land and laying out the allotments is only occasionally named in the act. There are a few examples in central southern England, such as William Walmesley in the act for Preston Candover (Hampshire) and Benjamin Price for West Knighton (Dorset), but in general the surveyor was regarded as a technician, working under the direction of the commissioners, and Parliament did not feel it necessary to know who he was. Indeed, many acts merely state that the commissioners shall have power to appoint a surveyor, and leave the matter entirely in their hands. A typical case is the Tangley (Hampshire) act of 1827, which allowed the sole commissioner, George Barnes, to appoint a surveyor if he felt it necessary. The assumption was almost certainly that Barnes, a highly experienced surveyor, would do the job himself, though as no award can now be found, it is not clear whether he actually did so.

The remaining parts of the acts consisted largely of general clauses listing the powers to be conveyed upon the officials and any specific clauses needed to deal with particular local circumstances. The general clauses rapidly assumed a more-or-less standard pattern, detailing the powers to stop up or create new roads and watercourses, specifying where copies of the award were to be deposited and laying out the financial arrangements to cover the costs of the process. Experienced agents, aware of which clauses had passed parliamentary scrutiny previously, simply copied these into each new act. The solicitor at Odiham quoted the Basingstoke act as justification for the proposed financial arrangements at Odiham, for example.[6] Those who were inexperienced merely borrowed copies of earlier successful acts, as one Yorkshire agent for Lord Ailesbury did from a Wiltshire counterpart.[7] This part of the procedure was greatly simplified by the 1801 General Inclosure Act, and acts after that date were able to refer to its standard clauses, greatly reducing their bulk.

Special local clauses are few, and are often deeply buried in the more general text, but they may be of considerable interest in revealing details of local customs or throwing light on the interests and obsessions of the characters involved. Many appear to have arisen from the inevitable horse-trading which had to take place in order for sufficient agreement to be reached to allow the bill to go ahead. One of the commonest is that a particular individual shall have a named piece of land as all or part of his share; another is that certain rights shall remain unaffected by the enclosure.

Though the acts were the ultimate authority for the enclosures, they are not necessarily either very precise or very accurate in the information they give. This is often deliberate, for the vast majority of enclosure acts were intended to enable the process to be carried out as quickly and efficiently as possible, and the last thing that was desired was that it should be brought to a halt by some technicality, which might require the trouble and expense of an amending act. It must also be realised that a substantial amount of time might pass between the act and the final completion of the enclosure, 47 years at Broad Chalke, and 35 at Wilton and Fugglestone (all Wiltshire), for example. Those named in the act may have played no part, or may have died long before the process came to an end. The four years between act and award at the Broyle enclosure in Ringmer was a sufficient period to see the deaths of four of the major players (Kay, 1979).

There are even cases where the act, though passed, appears never to have been implemented, and still more where they were implemented in part only. The Telscombe (Sussex) act provided for the enclosure of both open fields and downs, but when the final award was drawn up, the Sheep Down, consisting of 236 acres, was specifically left common, and the rights over it preserved exactly as before, with one minor adjustment. To determine what actually happened, it is therefore necessary to look at the awards.

The Awards

The enclosure awards and their associated maps are by far the most reliable source of information on what was actually done by any particular parliamentary enclosure, but they unfortunately do not always exist. Where an act was purely to give formal legal sanction to an enclosure which had already taken place, an award was not always felt to be necessary, though they were occasionally drawn up in such cases in order to ensure that there was a proper record of what had been confirmed. In the counties under consideration here, it appears that at least 18 parliamentary enclosures never had a formal award (see Appendix I). Fewer still ever had a map. Surveying and map-making were comparatively rare skills until well into the eighteenth century, and many early awards relied on identifying the allotments by the traditional method of describing their metes and bounds, in other words giving their size and what adjoined them on each side. Only gradually did it become accepted that it was essential to show these allotments on a map, and it has indeed been argued that it was the enclosure movement that forced the rapid development of the surveying profession.

Inevitably, some maps and awards which were made have subsequently been lost, though there is always the hope that a copy may reappear. In the case of Felpham (Sussex), the details of the enclosure were known only from a map until the Raper Papers were deposited in the West Sussex Record Office[8]. It may be hoped that the award for Tangmere (Sussex) for example might similarly come to light some day, for all that is currently available is an incomplete draft, though it appears that an award was actually formally completed.[9] There appears to be no evidence at all of an award for Tangley, though the act orders that one be drawn up and deposited with the Clerk of the Peace to the County, which was the most usual procedure.

Where an award exists, care must be taken to distinguish between the information given in the preamble and that which is listed under the individual allotments. The former is often merely a re-statement of the information given in the act, and hence suffers from the same level of inaccuracy. Where it differs, this is no guarantee that the award figure is any better. On occasions the act figure is closer to reality, though as suggested earlier, there is always the problem that the two figures may represent two different types of total.[10] Totals given at the end of the award may also be incorrect. It must be remembered that these had to be added up by hand, and that the division sums necessary to convert perches to roods and roods to acres (and even, occasionally, square yards to perches) were done in the same way. In the circumstances, it is hardly surprising that errors were sometimes made, and there was little real need to check the calculations. The total, after all, was of no great practical significance to those involved; their concern was with what they individually had been allotted, and how this compared with that allotted to their neighbours.

The format of the awards varies greatly, from an often highly complex and convoluted piece of continuous prose, to a simple tabulation. The latter became the norm only after 1845, and even then the allotments to the lord of the manor, any sales, and details of public allotments are usually hidden in a prose preamble. It is very easy to miss these in totalling the amount of land, and the totals given at the end of the table in the award itself usually omit them.

For the most part, the preambles consist of a re-statement of the terms of the act and an outline of the proceedings intended to demonstrate that what had been done was consistent with the act's clauses. They therefore add little that cannot be gleaned from other sources. However, they are the primary source of information about those who carried out the enclosure. Almost all begin with a greeting from the commissioners, thus establishing whether they are the same as those named in the act. If changes had been necessary, these are usually recited in detail, including the reasons for the absence of the original nominee and the procedures followed to appoint a replacement. The appointment of a surveyor may also be recorded here, but this is not always done, again reflecting the surveyor's subordinate status.

What all awards needed to contain was the person or persons to whom the land was being allocated, and an indication of which piece of land was intended (either by reference to metes and bounds or by a key to a map showing its location). They also almost invariably included the area of the plot, though this was not strictly necessary: early awards, in particular, were careful to specify 'be the same more or less', and it was the piece actually staked out on the ground which was the significant element. The tenure under which the land was held was also of considerable significance, since allotments claimed by virtue of property which was leasehold or copyhold became leasehold or copyhold themselves, and this was therefore normally noted in meticulous detail. The Tolpuddle (Dorset) award, for example, carefully distinguishes between the copyhold and leasehold allotments to William Vie, even though both were held from William Morton Pit.t.[11] The occasional failures to make these distinctions could lead to problems long after, as at Odiham, where various proprietors applied to the Inclosure Commissioners to have the award amended 68 years later because they were 'prejudiced by such inaccuracy'.[12]

The possibility of such legal confusion encouraged most commissioners to make separate allotments for each separate claim, so that an individual making multiple claims would receive a large number of allotments, often each individually of very small size. They were also apt to split claims to, for example, lordship of the manor, into several separate blocks, thus increasing still further the total number of plots. In practice, separate allotments to the same individual were often adjacent to each other, but in the absence of a map it is sometimes difficult to determine just how compact the pattern of land-holding became as a result of parliamentary enclosure.

Where all this basic information is present, the format in which it is given varies, and may not always be as helpful as it might be. In the Central Southern Counties it was normal to group all the allotments by holder, but grouping by the ultimate owner was sometimes adopted. In this latter case, the listing of a holder's leasehold, copyhold and freehold land would be scattered through the document. For example, the award for Sturminster Newton (Dorset) lists all lessees from the same owner together, so that Charles Newman, who leased land from Lord Rivers and from Mark Davis, in addition to owning land in his own right, appears at three different locations in the document.[13] Of more concern is the fact that, where a claimant died during the progress of an enclosure, the allotments were normally recorded as to 'the devisees of' that individual. Where these devisees held other land under their own names, this may give a distorted impression of the pattern of landholding, an issue which has been hotly debated in the literature. The ultimate expression of this was in a handful of awards where an allotment was made simply to 'the Owner'.[14]

Where enclosure maps exist, they may help to clarify some of these points, though they may in turn cause further problems. As has been indicated, early awards tended not to be accompanied by maps, though there are exceptions such as Dummer and Kempshot (Hampshire).[15] By the mid 1750s, however, it became normal to produce one showing the layout of the allotments, though this was not invariably the case. Pre-enclosure maps, showing the distribution of the holdings upon which the allotment was based are, unfortunately, quite rare, so it is not often possible to make direct comparisons of the before and after patterns, though private estate maps occasionally fill the gap. Those awards after 1845 usually record the land in respect of which an allotment is made in terms of the key numbers on the tithe map, so use of the two sources together may allow a direct comparison, though not all land was, of course, covered by the tithe documents.

The style of the maps varies greatly, from highly ornate (but not always accurate) maps of the whole parish or manor to a simple line plot showing the boundaries and key numbers of each allotment. In the latter case, locating the land may present difficulties, especially where there are a few isolated plots with few other features shown by which they can be identified. Such skeletal maps are a particular feature of the post-1845 period, and can be well illustrated by that of Piecombe (Sussex)[16].

Maps will immediately answer the question as to whether the multiple allotments to individuals really represent scattered holdings, or whether they form compact blocks. They may also help to explain some of the apparent scatter produced by the commissioners, for those that are more complete may show who owned the neighbouring already-enclosed land. From this, it can become obvious that the allotments were being attached to existing holdings of the owners concerned, which were outside the scope of the enclosure and which were themselves highly scattered.

Unfortunately, it is not unusual for discrepancies to occur between the maps and the awards. Acreages are sometimes given, either in a table on the map, or more frequently, on each individual parcel, and may differ from those in the accompanying text. Even the names of the owners may vary. At Walberton (Sussex), for example, a plot allotted to James Sayer in the award appears on the map as belonging to James Rusbridger. A change of name is often explicable by a change of ownership due to a sale or death between the drawing up of the two documents, but there is no doubt that errors crept in from time to time.

Various other documents, formal and informal, accompanied the enclosure process, but there was never any proper system for preserving them, so their survival is an even more chance matter than for the more formal record. In particular, many commissioners kept minute books of their proceedings, and Parliament eventually insisted on this, but it was never compulsory to retain them once the award had been completed, so many were no doubt simply scrapped. Those that remain may be a great source of insight into what actually happened, or may be a sore disappointment. The best list all the meetings, including who was present and precisely what action was taken. They may incorporate all the claims made and the objections to them, as well as the final decisions of the commissioners. They may also include details of specific requests, for example for an allotment to be placed next to the owner's existing property. A great deal of insight may be gained into the manoeuvring which inevitably accompanied such a major upheaval. The minute book for Portsmouth, for example, reveals a major dispute between the local farmers and the burgesses of Portsmouth.[17] Many extant minute books, however, are mere skeletal lists of meetings.

Commissioners' expenses fall into the same category as the minute books. Once the whole of the business was completed there seemed no reason to preserve them. Some do remain, sometimes even written in the minute book itself, and they are highly variable in the details which they record.

Locating records of parliamentary enclosures is a relatively straight-forward business. A complete collection of all the acts is contained in the House of Lords Record Office, and the British Library has an extensive, but not totally complete, collection. The latter, however, is technically of Bills, so it contains some which were subsequently modified in Parliament and even one or two which were never passed. This problem also applies to the collections held by the relevant county record offices: they, too, contain unmodified Bills, and some which failed to become law. These may be of considerable interest in themselves, since we know relatively little of the failures, but there is an obvious danger of taking information from the Bill on the assumption that this was what was finally implemented.

The locations of the awards is a less simple matter. Anything carried out under the authority of an Order, after 1845, had to be deposited with the Inclosure Commission in London, and a complete collection of these is in the Public Record Office. However, there were still some individual acts after this date, and there were still some awards under the 1836 act, neither of which necessarily involved such a deposit, so not all parliamentary enclosures of late date are there.

The situation is far worse for acts prior to 1845. The normal practice was to order that a copy should be enrolled with the Clerk of the Peace of the County, and such copies have now usually found their way into the county record office concerned. Unfortunately, none of the central southern counties possessed a Registry of Deeds, such as the Ridings of Yorkshire had, where all these documents were written up in bound volumes, so that the enrolled awards are often on individual sheets of parchment, which may have suffered damage over the intervening period. A common alternative to deposition with the Clerk was to deposit one instead in the parish church. These too have now usually been transferred to the record offices, but have also often suffered damage.

What complicates matters is that some acts made no specific provision for a deposit, and even when they did, it was not necessarily done. Responsibility for carrying out any instructions rested with the Clerks to the enclosures concerned, and these people, usually local solicitors, sometimes merely retained them amongst their own papers. Some have subsequently emerged, like that of Felpham, but it is from this source that more of the missing awards may one day appear. It is also possible that copies may be found in other collections. Often more than one copy of the award was made, and the lord of the manor or the tithe owner sometimes retained one, so that private estate papers or diocesan records may have them. These private copies may, however, cover only the individual's own land.

Where the Crown was involved, a further source is possible. Copies of at least those parts of the award relating to the Crown's rights and interests were sent to the relevant Crown office and these have now normally been deposited in the CREST collection of the Public Record Office. Unfortunately, the Crown's allotments were often the subject of a special separate award, and only this is preserved there, but in other cases a copy of the full text of the whole award was supplied. This seems sometimes to be the only copy which has survived, though no such example has been found from central southern England. However, the possibility exists that missing awards where the Crown was involved may turn up there, especially as all these entries are not indexed amongst the enclosures.

Formal Agreements

The Agreements

By definition, an enclosure by formal agreement must have had a written document detailing the terms under which the enclosure was to take place. Beyond that, it is extremely difficult to generalise, particularly as to what may be available now. Whereas all enclosure acts survive, in the House of Lords collection, if nowhere else, evidence of formal agreements may be forthcoming only through oblique references in other documents. Many were never deposited or registered formally with any official body, and therefore survive, if at all, in the private papers of one or other of the parties, or their agents or solicitors. An example is that of Abbotsbury (Dorset), which was preserved in the Fox-Strangeways archives, now deposited in the Dorset Record Office.[18] Where the agreement was an amicable arrangement between two or three landowners and the legal situation appeared to be crystal clear, there can have seemed little point in incurring the extra trouble and expense of placing a copy with the clerk of the peace, or in the courts of record. With the passage of time, the dying out of families and the break-up of estates has resulted in the loss of many of these privately held agreements, though others have found their way into the county record offices – not always the appropriate one for the agreement.[19]

Fortunately, some individuals felt the need to make formal deposits. More complex agreements, or those where there was an element of mistrust between the parties, would clearly encourage this, but in many cases the decision was no doubt determined by the cautious nature, or otherwise, of those involved. The increasing formality of the parliamentary process from the later eighteenth century onwards may also have encouraged a less cavalier attitude to what was, after all, legal evidence of individuals' willingness to surrender their rights over pieces of land.

The Awards

While relatively few parliamentary enclosures lack an award, the same is not true of formal agreements. A not-uncommon form of agreement was that certain individuals should be allowed to enclose some specified lands in exchange for the lord's right to enclose the rest. In such a case no award was necessary, since it was effectively contained within the agreement itself. Similarly, it was not unusual for the agreement to specify simply that the parties agreed to accept their portions of the land 'as staked out', for example at Winterborne Dauntsey (Wiltshire),[20] or that all should fence their existing holding in the common fields and surrender any rights to depasture stock over the rest. Again, the agreement itself was all that was required. Frequently in these cases the acreages of land remained unstated. If an individual agreed to accept land as staked out, or perhaps the whole of the North Common as his share, then there was no need to take the trouble to measure it.

At the other extreme, awards might be made which mimicked parliamentary ones in all their details. Later awards were often drawn up by commissioners and clerks accustomed to the local parliamentary format and, not surprisingly, they followed the pattern with which they were familiar. The awards for Frome Hill (Dorset) and for Bashley (Hampshire) could readily be mistaken for contemporary parliamentary examples. The details of the allottees, the acreage and the name of the location appear in the standard form. Such awards were normally enrolled in the court rolls or deposited with the clerks of the peace, like their parliamentary counterparts.

Between these two extremes, the extant awards span the whole range from sketchy scribbling on a scrap of paper to full listings in the local manorial court books. Acreages, if given, might be in customary or statute measure, and might vary from crude estimates to those which give every impression of being the product of a careful survey; names of fields or commons might be given in great detail, or might merely specify that 'the remainder' should go to a particular individual. Our knowledge of the details of formal agreements may thus vary wildly from one enclosure to another.

Informal Enclosures

The tracing of informal enclosures presents major difficulties on two counts. Firstly, by their very nature they cannot leave anything as concrete as an agreement or award, since if they did, they would be defined here as 'formal'. Secondly, since many were achieved in a piecemeal fashion, there is not one date of enclosure but many, and the final date, even if one could be established, would not necessarily be of any great significance. Only rarely do sources cover the whole of a parish in sufficient detail to give a picture of the total amount of land still under communal control at any one time, and it is equally rare to have a temporal sequence of records sufficiently close to pinpoint precisely when any individual plot was withdrawn. To expect to have both is to ask the impossible.

A further problem is that, since any individual 'enclosure event' rarely involved any immediate property reorganisation, it may be difficult to detect, even when the documents exist. Given the way that the process often appears to have operated, common rights may have effectively ceased at the moment when the tenant of a group of strips acquired the tenancy of the adjacent ones, though the significance of this may not have been apparent at the time. There is a considerable danger that anachronism may rule and, in the absence of any very striking physical change, references to, for example 'the Common Field', may persist after it has ceased to be common. Caution is therefore necessary, and often the best that can be achieved is a range of time during which a system, or parts of it, passed from being common and open to being enclosed.

It is impossible to cover in detail all the sources which might throw some light on the process. Private letters, diaries and odd notes scribbled by landowners or land agents may all contribute pieces to the jigsaw, and help to pinpoint particular phases in the process. There are, however, one or two more easily classifiable types of source which are worthy of attention. Prominent amongst these are glebe terriers, court books, leases and, of course, maps.

Glebe terriers can be an extremely valuable means of tracing informal enclosures, as Maurice Beresford pointed out many years ago (Beresford, 1948). In an ideal situation, glebe land, owned by the church for the support of the local priest, would be distributed in precisely the same way as the land of any other owner, with the same rights attached to it. If a parish had open fields, one might expect the glebe land to be scattered amongst them, and if it had any form of common grazing, one would expect such grazing rights to be attached to the glebe.

The diocesan authorities kept track of the land by requiring the churchwardens to make terriers (written surveys of the glebe) at varying intervals. It is thus possible, in theory, to follow the series through in date order to establish the point at which the land ceased to be listed as strips in the fields and became, instead, closes. Similarly, if a common pasture or waste were to be enclosed, this should be reflected in the disappearance of the rights from the terrier and their replacement in the next by land or a payment in lieu. Beresford even notes that a sudden change in the size of the terriers may be an indication, since an open-field terrier, with a great many small strips, is likely to be considerably bulkier than one covering two or three large closes.

In practice, glebe terriers are not always as helpful as it might seem, and on occasions they may even be totally misleading. To begin with, the series depends very much on the conscientiousness of both the diocesan authorities and the local churchwardens. If the former failed to demand terriers or the latter failed to respond, there may be long gaps between successive surveys, leaving a margin of error for the enclosure date of a century or more in some cases. Furthermore, some terriers seem simply to have been copied from the previous one, and it is not always clear whether the situation was really unchanged or the churchwardens were merely avoiding their duties. The possibility that a terrier was recording a situation which had long gone must be borne in mind, especially when dealing with a system where there was no formal enclosure.

A further problem is that the distribution of the glebe land did not necessarily reflect the general situation within the parish. The glebe frequently remained in scattered strips for some time after the rest of the field had been consolidated, since there were considerable doubts about the legal right of anyone to alienate the land, even in exchange for other land of equal or greater value. A landowner might thus be able to buy out or arrange exchanges with everyone else, but be powerless to reach agreement with the vicar and higher church authorities. However, it might be argued that in these circumstances the system still existed, albeit moribund, since technically the old communal rules would still apply. More seriously perhaps is the alternative case, where the glebe was for one reason or another in closes, while other owners retained strips in fully functioning common fields, or more frequently, where common rights existed in which the glebe had no part. It is all too easy in these circumstances to assume that no system existed, and abandon the search for further evidence.

Finally, it may be noted that not all parishes had glebe land, particularly by the eighteenth century, and that even if they did, terriers did not always record it. A large number of mid-eighteenth century terriers from the Lincoln Diocese make no mention of land, even though earlier and later ones for the same parishes make clear that such land existed.

In spite of these difficulties glebe terriers remain one of the most accessible means of pinpointing an enclosure. They provide a chronological sequence of snapshots of a highly stable landholding, since the glebe was not normally subject to sale, alienation, or confiscation as other lands were, and the impact of enclosure is therefore relatively easy to identify. Indeed, the churchwardens sometimes felt obliged to explain the changes by noting, for example, that the lands they record had been received in exchange 'at the recent enclosure', or similar phrases.

Manorial Court Books are a highly variable but potentially very useful source. Much depends on the extent to which the particular manor was a functioning entity at the time concerned, and inevitably, it was often precisely when the manor ceased to be effective that enclosure took place. Frustratingly, the last entry in the court book is often the last record of an apparently fully operational system; the next record, from whatever other kind of source may be available, shows it gone.

Two aspects of the court's work tend to be of value in this context. Firstly, the court was responsible for enforcing the law regarding common rights and it was here that offenders were prosecuted. Presentations for encroachment may well provide a comprehensive picture of the disappearance of a common, or the fencing off of portions of the common fields. Often the same individuals are prosecuted time and time again for the same offence, and it is clear that the court is merely recording its failure to stem the encroaching tide.

Secondly, the court was responsible for the admission of 'manorial tenants', for example copyholders. A change in tenancy, due for example to the death of a holder, or to a woman wishing to transfer a holding to her future husband, would be registered by the court, and such registrations may reveal significant changes in the nature of the holding. The sudden omission of references to associated common rights or of the phrase 'in the common field called…' may point to a recent enclosure. Unfortunately, detailed descriptions of such customary holdings were often felt to be unnecessary, and a bare statement that someone had been admitted to 'the copyhold known as…' may be all that appears.

Sequences of leases, where they exist, may be a far better guide. Since leases were not customarily defined holdings, there was a need to specify in detail precisely what the lease covered, and in consequence, as with glebe terriers, it is usually relatively easy to detect land scattered in open fields and any common rights associated with it. By extension, the next lease after enclosure reveals the changes which have taken place. What is often far less clear is whether this represented a general enclosure, or merely the piecemeal withdrawal of the leased land from the system.

The ultimate evidence of the open or enclosed state of an area is the map. Estate maps almost invariably distinguish in some way between land which is fenced and that

3. Portland open fields. Unploughed baulks mark the divisions between the properties.

which is not, most frequently by using solid or dotted lines for the property boundaries, and most add extra information about the land's status, either by naming the common fields as such on the map itself, or by providing this information in a key. In this context, even a partial map, showing for example a single scattered holding, can be far more informative than a written lease for the same area. Documentary evidence of, say, ten acres of strips 'in the West Field' would give little indication of the extent of the fields as a whole, while a map showing the distribution of the strips will at worst offer a pointer to its minimum extent (see Map 2). Maps also indicate field *shape*, and while this in itself can never be regarded as totally conclusive, the existence of the characteristic strip form is at least a warning of the possible presence and location of an open field, either extant or recently defunct.

Where open fields or commons survived into the mid nineteenth century, the documents of the tithe commutation process in the late 1830s and early 1840s provide by far the most comprehensive evidence. Since piecemeal enclosure by its very nature almost never involved any arrangements for commuting tithes, it is precisely those parishes affected by this process which are most likely to have a complete tithe cover. The national survey of the tithe documentation by Kain and Oliver (1995) draws attention to many degraded systems which can be detected from the tithe maps, and use of map and apportionment together can often fill in details of such survivals, for example their names and precise extent, in a way which is not possible from any other source. The remnant narrow unenclosed strips at Eastbourne and Brighton, interspersed with similar-shaped but enclosed ones, provide graphic evidence of the piecemeal process in operation in the southern counties.[21]

The tithe documents may also point to the timing of the changes. If enclosure involved changes in boundaries or land-use, it was liable to affect the tithe rent charge on the properties and henceforce the formality of an amended apportionment. The

4. South Downs at Treyford Hill. A regular landscape produced by enclosure from the downs by a large estate.

re-apportionment at Burleston (Dorset) in 1860 seems to have been just such a case, though the enormous contrast between that map and the almost classic open field layout of the original of 1843 suggests that some undiscovered formal agreement may have been put into effect here.

In the final analysis, it is often not the absence of records which is the main problem, but the difficulties in interpreting those which exist. The problems of anachronisms have already been discussed, but locating and identifying the lands involved may create far greater problems. Though there were fields and commons with highly unusual names, such as 'Pepperstick Field' (Crondall, Hampshire) or 'Bibkledge Field' (Charlton Marshall, Dorset), many of the former bore simple locational names such as 'North' or 'Middle', while amongst the latter those such as 'Cow Common' or 'Oxpasture' abounded. Hampshire, for example, had some forty-five 'North Fields' and a dozen 'Cow Downs', plus a 'Cow Down Field'. In a document covering several manors or townships it may be by no means clear which 'North Field' had been recently enclosed. Wiltshire, in particular, had a good many parishes with several independent field systems within them, and these often shared at least one or two of their names.

The difficulties are increased by the fluid nature of many of the fields in the central southern counties. Fields might be subdivided or combined, and in either case the whole or a part of a field might be involved, with or without additions of land from elsewhere. In Portsmouth, Fountain Field gained the alternative name 'Dock Field' in the early sixteenth century as a result of the growth of Henry VII's dockyard, which adjoined it. When it was later split into East Dock and West Dock Fields the name 'Fountain Field' was retained as a synonym for 'East Dock Field' only. West Dock Field proved short-lived, being rapidly overwhelmed by the expansion of the dockyard and the creeping encroachment of housing, and effectively ceased to exist in 1710. East Dock Field underwent some extension at the expense of the adjacent common, but the name 'Fountain' gradually fell into disuse, being replaced by yet another synonym, 'Pesthouse Field', after the building of an isolation hospital in 1693. 'East Dock' and 'Pesthouse' continued to be used interchangeably until the final fragments were built upon in the late 1830s and early 1840s. Strangely, the older name is preserved in 'Fountain Street', part of the encroaching urban area.

The confusing multiplicity of names for this field was by no means unique. In Portsmouth itself, two other fields had alternative names, Town Field being also known as Mere, and Meteland having two synonyms, Cherry Garden and Kingston. Portsmouth's strategic importance ensured a great wealth of documentation and maps which enable these complexities to be unravelled. Other places present a more difficult problem. At Seagry (Wiltshire) the fields were referred to as 'East', 'North', and 'West' in 1585, but in 1656 as 'North', 'Down', and 'Clay Corner' (VCH, XIV, 191). The relationship of these two groups to each other is not entirely clear, since various changes certainly took place before their final disappearance in 1710. The confusion is compounded by the habit of describing the fields by the crop which was in them, a description which would obviously change from year to year. Portsmouth records frequently refer to the Barley Ersh'[22] and the 'Wheat Ersh', rather than the proper names, and a similar habit occurred in the other counties, for example at Marden (Wiltshire).

Reorganisations similar to those at Portsmouth were not unusual. For example, the three fields of West Grimstead (Wiltshire) were divided into four by an agreement of 1726, forty acres being taken from the down and added to the fields at the same time.[23] It was agreed that the new fields were to be named 'Pott Furlong Field', 'Kitehill Field', 'Redland Field' and 'East Field', but by the enclosure of 1802-5 these had become five, 'East', 'West', 'Middle', 'Inner Down' and 'Outer Down' Fields.[24] In the intervening period, incidentally, there are references to the 'Barley Field'.

It must be stressed that the mass of sources available for Portsmouth is almost unique, and a similar volume of documentation is hardly ever to be found elsewhere. Few rural villages were adequately mapped before the second half of the eighteenth century, and few compilers of contemporary documents saw any reason to record what was perfectly obvious to them unless disputes arose which needed formal legal action. In consequence, open and common lands are easily missed, and double counting of systems is also highly probable. In general, however, it would seem far more likely that remnants of common land which survived undetected to a late date would more than counterbalance any double recording.

Conclusion

One of the inevitable consequences of these great variations in the nature of the sources is that the estimates of the extent of the different types of enclosure are subject to widely differing degrees of error. For parliamentary enclosures, the fact that only a handful of awards are unavailable and that almost all give figures with at least some degree of both precision and accuracy, means that we can be reasonably certain of the totals. For formal agreements, the margin of error is far greater; in many individual examples, the level of accuracy may be as high, or even higher, than for those by act, but the absence of figures from so many others, or even the absence of any award at all, means that the overall totals for this method are at best of the right order of magnitude.

The major problem rests with the informal enclosures. Not only are any totals liable to be out by a considerable order of magnitude, but the balance between the different types of land is likely to be highly distorted. Understatement of the acreage of common, as compared with open field, is almost inevitable. By the eighteenth century, holdings in fields were generally assigned an acreage, and while these might not approximate very closely to statute acres, and customary acres might vary substantially locally, they provide some indication of size. Holdings in fields were usually carefully recorded when they changed hands, and they were far more likely to be carefully mapped, if the occasion arose to map the village at all. Commons, on the other hand, tend to leave little precise record until a far later date. Stinted commons might be referred to in terms of the number of beastgates held by any individual, but the beastgate was simply a measure of the supposed carrying capacity, which varied wildly according to the nature of the land, and which in any case might be altered from time to time as that supposed capacity was reassessed.[25] For unstinted commons even that dubious information is normally lacking.

The discrepancy is made worse by the fact that any open field which is recorded can be confidently listed as having been subsequently enclosed, with the sole exception of the Portland (Dorset) system. For commons, only those which *wholly* disappeared can be so listed, and even then, only if there is no possibility that they survive under alternative names. For the great many commons which still exist, only a direct reference to part being enclosed can suffice as evidence, a much higher level of proof than is needed for the fields.

One very crude indicator of the relative importance of the different methods is simply to calculate the percentage of 'elements' finally abolished by each means. 'Elements', in this context, must be taken to mean each set of common fields, common meadows, or common pastures and wastes run as a separate entity; depending on local circumstances, this 'entity' might be a parish, manor, township or tithing. It must be emphasised that this does not involve counting each enclosure 'event', but only the method of final abolition. This method will obviously understate the informal element since, as will be demonstrated later, many elements which were finally abolished by act or formal agreement had already been extensively reduced by informal means; in the case of commons, they might still exist today, in spite of centuries of informal enclosure. However, the 'Enclosure Index', as this indicator will be termed, does at least serve as a rough comparative measure both for the different types of land within a county and for comparisons between counties.

The problems outlined above need to be borne in mind when approaching the various totals offered in this book. It is highly likely that informal enclosure is underestimated, and even more so that the acreage of common land enclosed is understated. It is also likely that many informally enclosed fields or commons survived rather longer than is indicated. In a great many cases, all one can say is that they still existed at a particular date, and there is no justification for assuming that they survived any later. However, to assume that in each case the last chance reference immediately preceded their final disappearance is clearly ludicrous. To demand precise dates and acreages is to seek a precision which the sources do not permit.

4

Dorset

Dorset has traditionally been regarded as the south-western corner of a triangle of 'open field' counties, the other 'corners' being Sussex and Yorkshire. Crude though this concept is, it does offer a starting point for the discussion of enclosure in the county. Much of Dorset consists of compact villages which, at some time in their history, have contained communally controlled open field systems, in contrast to the counties to the west where hamlets and scattered farms have tended to dominate and open fields, where they existed, tended to be small and a relatively minor part of the agricultural system. As a further crude generalisation, it might be expected that townships in the west of Dorset, towards the Devon border, would be more likely to have lacked open fields, or lost them early, than those elsewhere in the county. A glance at map 5 confirms this pattern, for open fields were largely missing from the far western part of the county by 1700.

Closer inspection reveals other elements to the pattern. Systems tended to be few in the north-west of the county, where extensive heathlands dominated the landscape and where the existence of Cranborne Chase had superimposed a human check on an already physically unpromising environment. Villages here, where they existed, tended not to have open field systems, at least by 1700. The same is also true of the eastern part of the Isle of Purbeck and of the north-central part of the county. In these cases there is some evidence that systems had existed but been lost to earlier enclosure, though the details of this are beyond the scope of this study. The other major blank in the pattern represents the extensive heaths around and westwards from Poole Harbour. Here the situation is a little different, in that there were few villages to contain any field systems. The heaths themselves, however, were often the target of attempts to reclaim additional farmland, so the absence of open fields should not be taken as indicative of an absence of enclosure. As will be discussed later, much of Dorset's enclosure was of common and waste rather than fields.

In total, 117 open field systems seem to have been operating in 1700, and three others, Batcombe, Southover in Frampton, and Powerstock, have left evidence of their existence from the 1690s, but no indication as to precisely when they disappeared. A further system lying in the parish of Buckland Newton was enclosed by agreement in 1699, as was Morden in 1695. In other words, just under half [1] of

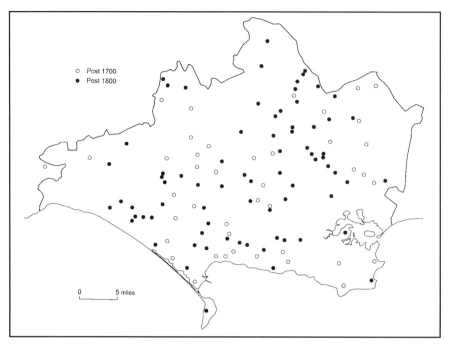

5. Localities with surviving open fields in Dorset in 1700 and 1800.

Dorset's parishes contained open fields at the beginning of the eighteenth century. Of these, 74, or approximately 64 per cent, were still in existence in 1800. As has been discussed in an earlier chapter, this does not necessarily mean either that there were 116 textbook systems in 1700 or that 74 remained unchanged over the succeeding century. Dorset certainly possessed systems which bore a close resemblance to the classic model, and some of these survived in that form into the nineteenth century, for example at Winterborne Kingston, but, as in much of the country, systems tended to be variable in their details and much more fluid in their make-up than the classic model would assume. Partial enclosure of systems, even of substantial parts, was by no means unusual, while other parts of the same system continued to be farmed in common. Fontmell Magna, for example, retained remnants of fields until the 1840s though most was already enclosed by 1774,[2] and Nether Compton was partly enclosed by the early eighteenth century but retained remnant fields until 1863.[3]

The position as far as common and waste is concerned is more difficult to ascertain. It was even more susceptible to quiet encroachment than the fields, and lords were often only too happy to accept this, providing rent was paid. Formal records of enclosure thus represent a very much greater understatement than for fields. Furthermore, Dorset commons were wildly variable in size, from one or two acres to many hundreds, and are easily overlooked in the records for any particular time period. In contrast to open fields, it seems highly likely that virtually all Dorset parishes had at least some common at some time, and apart from some specific dramatic event, such as the emparking of Leweston or the desertion of the whole village as at Winterbourne Clenston, most might have been expected to retain them, possibly in an attenuated form, into the seventeenth century at least. These commons undoubtedly underwent further erosion before 1700, but only occasionally do they seem to have been completely eliminated. In some cases, a formal agreement resulted in a whole common being enclosed, as at Bradpole in 1593,[4] but frequently the parish or township concerned had other commons which were not affected. By 1700, it seems that 132 townships or other separate agricultural entities retained some common. A substantial majority of Dorset's communities were thus involved in some form of commons enclosure during the two centuries under consideration, in spite of the continued existence of much common into the twentieth century.

A final comment must be offered on the position of common meadow in the county. Though limited in extent by comparison with the other two categories of common land, common meadows certainly played a significant role in the agricultural economy of Dorset in the early part of the eighteenth century, and continued late into the nineteenth century in some localities. The problems of identification have been covered elsewhere,[5] and these apply with full force to Dorset. Confusion of names, and a strong tendency to use informal means of enclosure obscure the picture. However, at least forty parishes or townships had common meadows in 1700 and one other meadow, at Kingston Maureward, is recorded in 1699 and very probably continued into the following century. Exactly half of the forty were still in existence in 1800, and at least four are recorded as surviving into the 1960s (Stamp and Hoskins, 1963, pp.267-270).

There is good evidence that many continued to be used in common, as opposed to merely remaining open, into the nineteenth century, and the use of the term 'Changeable Acre' at Woodsford implies the continuation of periodic redistribution of the strips amongst the proprietors in the eighteenth, as was certainly the case in Sussex. Certainly rules could be highly complex, as at West Holme, Stockford and Rushton, where some lands of Stockford Farm had full rights in Rushton Meadow, but only foreshares in Holme Meadow and foreshares every other year in Haywards Hams. Conversely, East Holme estate had only the afterfeed in West Holme Meadow.[6]

The Background to Enclosure

The enclosure process in Dorset was much influenced by the dominance of large estates over a substantial part of the county. Families such as the Draxes of Charborough Park, the Welds of Lulworth and the Pitt Rivers held sway over great tracts of territory and all, or almost all, of a good many parishes lay in the hands of a single owner, leaving the individual concerned able to enclose almost at will. There was often little need to invoke the powers of Parliament, since even if there were another minor owner, it may well have been possible either to reach an agreement to enclose or to ignore the common rights which nominally still existed. A typical case appears to have been Burleston where, in 1843, one William Pole Tynley Long Wellesley, Esquire, owned all but 1.4 acres of the parish, this last being the glebe land which the rector held in hand. Wellesley let the whole of his almost 350 acres to one individual, Amey Collier, who was presumably able to farm as he wished, without the formality of an enclosure. By 1860, Wellesley's land had become split between George James Wood and Major-General Sir John Michel, and a reorganisation of the whole parish into large compact blocks was felt necessary. This in turn necessitated a reapportionment of the tithe rent charge between the new fields, thus providing a formal record of events.[7]

Burleston was a classic case, in that the stumbling block to an earlier enclosure by agreement was the existence of the glebe. In view of the legal doubts about the right of a rector to conclude an agreement for exchange of the glebe which would be binding on his successors, Wellesley and the rector would have been obliged to obtain an act in order to be certain of their future titles to the exchanged lands. Such a course cannot have seemed economic, since Wellesley and his tenant must already have had an almost free hand. Had the rector been willing to let to Collier, and had not Wellesley's land been subdivided, there might never have been any need to upset the *status quo*, and Burleston might have left no record of the final disappearance of its fields. In practice, by 1860 the parties obviously felt a formal arrangement was advisable, and legislative changes had by then opened the way for an enforceable agreement between the parties.

In earlier times there was little option but to go for an act, as at Compton Valence. Once more there was only one owner, Morton Pitt, plus the Rector, but when, in 1808, they decided to enclose, an act was obtained to make the arrangements legally watertight. This was occasionally done even in the second half of the nineteenth century. At Warmwell, a very similar case to Burleston, formal parliamentary procedures were felt necessary as late as 1868. Over ninety per cent of the open land, almost 548 acres, was owned jointly by Augustus Foster and Augustus Billet Foster, but the remaining 50 acres was held by the Rector, Rev. Edward Cambridge. Whether it proved impossible for Cambridge and the Fosters to reach an agreement, or whether they were concerned that a future Rector might renege on the deal is not clear, but a parliamentary Order was sought under the 1845 General Act, and a formal award drawn up by an independent valuer, James Rawlence of Bulbridge.[8]

While such single-owner dominance was not unusual in the county, it nevertheless applied only to a minority of the area. In most parishes there were at least two or three minor freeholders, and often quite substantial areas of a parish were in the hands of other individuals. It was by no means necessary for the lord to be the principal landowner, and there might be more than one manor involved, even if there was only a single field system. In these circumstances, some form of accommodation had to be reached with the other parties. At the lowest level, as has been stressed, it was often possible for an individual to withdraw his land or enclose portions of a common with no more than the tacit agreement of the other parties. Far greater security rose from either a formal written agreement with them or, as a last resort, an Act of Parliament.

It must also be remembered that other individuals were involved apart from the land-*owners*, and that large-scale ownership by one individual was not necessarily any guarantee that an act could be avoided, as a number of cases in Dorset make clear. Quite apart from the possibility of conflicting attitudes amongst the freeholders, there was also the possible stumbling block provided by the various land-*holders*. At Bere Regis, for example, Jane Ernle Drax was technically the 'reversioner' (i.e. the ultimate owner) of almost 84 per cent of the land, but 296 acres (16.9 per cent) was leased out to no fewer than 14 individuals, and a further 239 acres (13.6 per cent) was in the hands of eight copyholders. One, Thomas Spear, was both a leaseholder and a copyholder, and also incidentally a freeholder, in respect of different parts of his holding. These 21 holders were all parties to the enclosure, and their rights could no more be legally over-ridden than those of the owners. This is not to imply that they were necessarily against an enclosure, but unscrambling the holdings in such a way that everyone felt satisfied would have been an extraordinarily difficult task, and Drax found it necessary or prudent to obtain an act.[9]

A similar situation faced Lord Rivers at Sturminster Newton. Rivers owned 363 acres, just over 83 per cent of the land involved, but over 150 acres was leased to 52 individuals.[10] At the moment of enclosure therefore, Rivers effectively controlled less than half the land, and to achieve an enclosure by agreement he would have had to produce a redistribution which satisfied all 52, as well as the 28 other owners and another individual who was leasing land from one of the 28. At the start of the process the numbers involved were even greater, for Rivers bought out ten owners while the enclosure was under way, as well as buying part of the land of an eleventh.[11] The prospect of getting 92 individuals to accept any solution as fair must have been a daunting one, and it would be quite wrong to assume, as is sometimes done, that the others concerned were necessarily poor peasant farmers who could be easily overawed. One seller, for example, was John Chichester, esquire.

Parliamentary Enclosure

The parliamentary enclosures of Dorset were the subject of a thesis some sixty years ago, though this covered only the period up to 1837, and effectively omitted those under the 1836 and 1845 General Enclosure Acts (Endacott, 1938, p. 4). This work also omitted both the Radipole and Cranborne Chase enclosures on the grounds that neither was a true enclosure. Both, however, are similar in nature to those usually regarded as enclosures in other counties, and are listed by authorities such as Turner (1978): they have therefore been included as parliamentary here. Their inclusion accounts for some of the discrepancies between the totals quoted here and those given by Endacott. Another source of the differences is that Endacott excludes all exchanges, but includes the areas of roads, while the opposite decision has been adopted in this work, to accord with the pattern used for the National Enclosure Project.

Altogether, there were 106 enclosures either by individual act or under the authority of the General Acts from 1836 onwards. Of these, two, those for East Lulworth and Coombe Keynes and for Tarrant Keynston, were confirmatory of enclosures which had already taken place by agreement, and it seems highly likely that West Stour was similar, for the act there named 'referees' (to determine any disputes) rather than 'commissioners' (who had power to carry out the whole enclosure themselves). The East Lulworth and Combe Keynes was only partially confirmatory, in that the act enclosed some open areas, but was used as an opportunity to give additional legal backing to an existing enclosure by agreement.

The acreage involved is difficult to assess precisely. No award appears to exist for four of the enclosures, Gillingham and Motcombe, Radipole, West Stour, and Tarrant Keynston, and it is unlikely that any ever did exist for the last three, for the form of the enclosure made one unnecessary. That for Gillingham and Motcombe cannot now be found, though a reference in a document of 1818 appears to indicate that one was made, and that allotments were laid out in the normal way. The acreage for Radipole was almost certainly so small as to make no significant difference to the total, and that for Tarrant Keynston, given as 169 acres in the act, is probably reasonably accurate, but the West Stour and Gillingham act figures have all the appearance of highly rounded guesses. In view of the comments earlier[12] they must be regarded with considerable suspicion.

Three sets of figures are available as a guide. Professor Michael Turner's (1978 and 1980) calculations, based on the award and act estimates, give a total of 94,078 acres, or almost exactly 15 per cent of the county area.[13] Endacott, using a slightly different basis for calculation, gives an estimated total of 76588 by private act plus 7571 under the General Act of 1836 and a further 9733 under that of 1845, an overall total of 93,892 acres, or 14.8 per cent (Endacott, pp. 19-20). Our own figures, incorporating additions of the individual allotments for 14 of the awards (less Cranborne Chase and Radipole) give 91,694.05 acres, or 14.66 per cent. The closeness of these estimates is at first sight encouraging, and suggests that probably just under 94,000 acres, or 15 per cent of the county area, was enclosed by parliamentary means. Unfortunately the presence or absence of the very large Cranborne Chase enclosure throws some doubt on the apparent convergence of the figures. If that part of the Cranborne Chase award which applies to Dorset[14] is added, our own total is raised to 103,137.92 acres, or 16.49 per cent, and adding this same amount to Endacott's figures would raise his total to 105,336 acres, or 16.84 per cent. The discrepancy with Turner's figures arises because he, in the absence of any act or award estimate, seems to use the average of the other enclosures in a county to supply the deficit; unfortunately the mean for Dorset is only 888 acres, leading to a substantial underestimate on Cranborne Chase. Adjusting for the correct figure raises Turner's total to 104,634 acres, in the same range as our own and Endacott's.

A more contentious issue is the type of land involved. Turner (1980, p.178) divides acts into those which contained open field and those which did not, and quotes these totals for Dorset as 51872 acres and 42206 acres respectively.[15] Unfortunately this has led to assumptions, nationally at least, that open field dominated the enclosure movement. This is not so. The fact that an enclosure involved some open field is no indication whatsoever that that was the dominant type of land, and very frequently it was not. Of the random sample of eleven awards mentioned earlier, seven contained open field and four did not, a proportion which coincides exactly with the proportions in Turner's figures.[16] However, in the seven which did, the amount of common and waste exceeded that of field in five: in only two was field land dominant. Only one Dorset award, that for Trent, seems to have been concerned solely with enclosing open field,[17] though occasionally the amount of common was minimal, as, for example, at Tolpuddle.[18] To add further to the confusion, the award for Mosterton, which Turner records as containing open field, covered only common meadow.

More realistically, the ten per cent sample gives the proportions of field as 34.18 per cent to 60.29 per cent of pasture and waste. Additionally there was 1.75 per cent of common meadow and 3.78 per cent of redistributed old enclosed land. While the sample was intended to be part of a national sample and is not large enough to give totally accurate figures for Dorset, there is little doubt from inspection of most of the other awards that the balance between field and pasture is of the right order of magnitude. Endacott unfortunately does not offer any over-all figure, and those which he does quote are intended to offer a picture of enclosure in specific areas, rather than a representative sample of the whole. However, it is interesting that his analysis of 13 chalkland parishes, where open field would be expected to dominate the process if it did anywhere, nevertheless shows a slight excess of pasture over field, 52.3 per cent to 47.6. There would seem to be little doubt that a significant majority of Dorset's parliamentary enclosure was concerned with common and waste.

According to the normal definition, the whole parliamentary enclosure movement had its origins in Dorset, at Radipole in 1603. This enclosure is admittedly something of an oddity, as were all of those in the seventeenth century, since the purpose in this case was merely to allow for the building of a chapel on common ground. However, unlike the rather similar Portsea case of 1753, it has a claim to be a genuine enclosure, since it did involve the removal of part of the common for private purposes and the abolition of rights over that area. Its unique status is emphasised by the fact that there were no further enclosure acts in the county for over a hundred years. As will be discussed later, enclosure certainly went on in the intervening period, but by other means. The two acts in the 1730s may also be regarded as something of a false start, since they were not followed up for a further 25 years, when the acts for Langton Herring and East Lulworth and Coombe Keynes were passed. Effectively, as fig. 6 shows, it was not until the 1760s that a steady trickle of bills began to be presented.

From then onwards, the temporal pattern up to the 1820s followed the one made familiar at a national level by writers such as Turner (1980) and Mingay (1997). The low level of the 1770s and 1780s was suddenly boosted in the succeeding decades by the impact of the Napoleonic Wars, with an equally sudden fall when the economic stimulus of the wars was removed. Thereafter Dorset went its own way. A good deal of open field land still remained in the county in the 1820s, and the passing of the

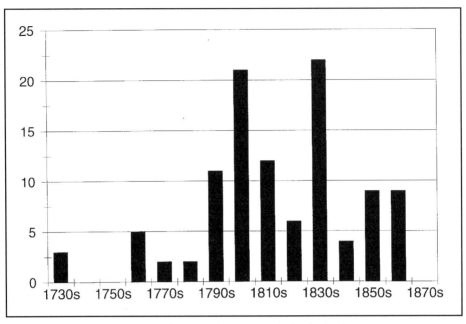

6. Timing of Dorset enclosure acts and orders by decade.

General Act of 1836 presented the ideal opportunity to tackle these in a relatively inexpensive way. No less than sixteen awards were made under this legislation, and, when the various individual private acts are added in, it would appear at first glance that the 1830s were the peak period for parliamentary enclosures. In fact this is somewhat misleading. Though the 1836 act was the authority for so many enclosures, only one of them, for Briants Puddle, was completed in that decade, and there is nothing to suggest that the others were begun then. The earliest of the rest, Bagber in Sturminster Newton, was not completed until 1844, and six were carried out in the 1850s. While the act was therefore of especial importance to Dorset, its full impact was substantially delayed.

The other observable late peak in the 1850s and 1860s is less unusual, since it was a feature of a good many counties outside the Midland belt. However, the 1845 General Act again had a particular significance for Dorset, which still possessed many commons which were either small or of doubtful agricultural value, or both. Only when this legislation had simplified and cheapened the process must it have seemed worthwhile to tackle some of these. According to Turner's figures, seven of the twenty-two awards under the 1845 act involved less than 100 acres, with the smallest, Margaret Marsh, covering a mere 13, and this emerges clearly if the acreage, rather than the number of acts, is considered (see fig. 7). It is worth noting that three were also concerned with open field. As late as 1868 Warmwell field, of just under 190 acres, was enclosed by this means, together with 409 acres of heath and common.

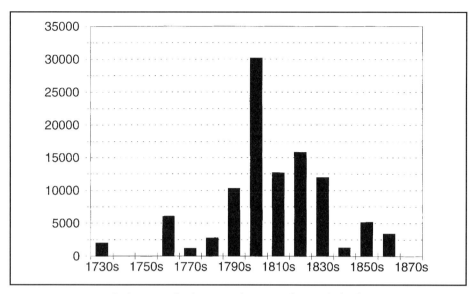

7. Acreages enclosed in Dorset by act or order in each decade.

The spatial pattern of parliamentary enclosure in the county shows a close resemblance to that of the distribution of open field systems in 1700, though it must not therefore be assumed that the former was concerned largely with the latter (see fig. 8). West of a line through Bridport and Beaminster parliamentary enclosures were lacking, apart from the small late commons enclosure at Mosterton. They were also sparse in the north-west of the county, along the Somerset border, and their relative dearth along the Hampshire border reflects the low density of villages amongst the heathlands mentioned earlier. In the latter case the lack of numbers is partly counteracted by the large size of some of the few heathland enclosures which took place there, such as the 11,403-acre Canford Magna enclosure. Heathlands were also highly susceptible to small-scale informal encroachment, an aspect which will be discussed later.

Early enclosures, prior to the outbreak of the Napoleonic Wars, were largely close to the coast, including the port of Wareham, a not-unexpected pattern in a county which was at the time economically backward and lacked any of the newly developing major industries. Only those parts with ready access to transport links to external markets had any major incentive to incur the expenses of an act. After 1793, however, no particular patterns seem discernable. There is no sign of a link between either simple spatial location or soil type and the date at which enclosure took place. As in many other counties, at a detailed level the prime determining factor seems to have been personalities and the tenurial pattern within an individual parish.

Failed attempts to obtain an act ran at roughly the national average. Throughout England as a whole approximately one in five bills presented to Parliament failed to become acts and Dorset's 19 failures matches this quite closely. Again, as is typical nationally, the majority of these 'failures' were in fact no more than temporary set-

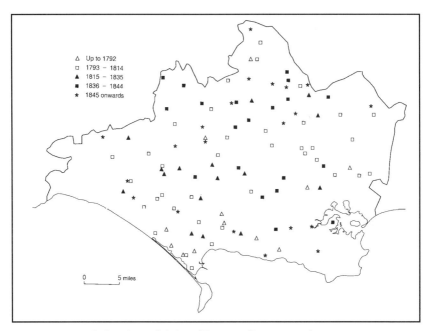

8. Location and timing of Dorset parliamentary enclosures.

backs, often due to minor defects in the bill or the procedures which had been followed. However, seven were rather more serious, and in two cases, Holnest and Fordington, no act was ever obtained. The most spectacular delay was at Upwey, where 89 years elapsed between the initial attempt to obtain an act in 1745 and final success in 1834. A similar order of delay was experienced at Charminster, delayed for 61 years until 1830, and at Fordington, discussed in more detail later, where it took over 40 years to achieve an agreement and the final stages took place over 70 years later. Chesilbourne and Holnest both had to wait more than 30 years for their enclosures, the former under the General Act of 1836, the latter by agreement.

Some successful bills also faced formal opposition in Parliament before they were passed. Five acts, those for Lytchett Matravers, Owermoigne, Piddletrenthide, Sydling St Nicholas, and Winfrith Newburgh, had counter-petitions lodged against them, but in these cases Parliament over-rode the opposition. This is not entirely surprising, since most would-be enclosers had the sense to test out the opposition before going as far as to present a bill to Parliament. The whole process was an expensive one, and there was little point in going ahead unless the chances of success seemed good. As a consequence, the formal proceedings at most enclosures were preceded by much informal contact aimed at determining who was prepared to support such a move and at persuading, cajoling, or occasionally threatening potential opposition.

An illustration of the behind-the-scenes manoeuvring which was often necessary to obtain an enclosure is provided by the collection of papers which have survived for Beer Hackett.[19] The area was quite small, just under 59 acres, and there were only nine claimants with 26 'leazes' (rights to turn out stock) between them. The first evidence of interest was a notice of 21 September 1842 calling a meeting for 10 October, and signed by John Redway, Thomas Fooks and John Vincent. A further meeting followed on 24 March 1843, at which six of the parties were represented and passed a resolution to seek an enclosure, and in a letter of 12 April Edward Percy accepted the post of commissioner.[20] On 7 October a notice appeared in the Western Flying Post, Sherborne and Yeovil Journal advertising the first formal meeting at which claims to rights in the land were to be submitted.

The intention was to enclose under the authority of the 1836 General Act and this proved the first stumbling block. William Hawker Helyar, alone of the owners, refused his consent on the grounds that he would lose his timber rights. Helyar held only five of the leazes, so the condition in that act that two-thirds must be in favour was easily met, but Helyar was also lord of one of the manors, and legal opinion had to be sought as to whether the others could go ahead in the face of his opposition. A Mr Batten also expressed opposition, provoking an angry response from Edward Percy, who stated that 'he sees thro' a lens so opaque as not to be able to discover benefit to the Land Owners or Occupiers' in a letter to William Fooks, clerk to the enclosure and another member of the Sherborne firm of solicitors, Fooks Goodden. It is not clear precisely how this opposition was overcome, though there may well have been some private deal between Helyar and Digby, for the latter bought out Helyar's allotment at the enclosure.

A further problem struck the enclosure when Edward Percy died. Percy was an active commissioner in the area, and his death left four enclosures in temporary limbo. Percy died on 12 January 1848, but it took until 31 July 1850 to hold a formal meeting to replace him. Meanwhile, William Haggett had been carefully lobbying for the post, writing to Fooks to say that he had all Percy's papers and 'As I have in every instance been appointed to succeed him I trust in this case to receive the same favour'. His wish was granted, and it was Haggett who finally signed the completed award on 5 March 1853, over ten years after the first formal moves had been made.

A more complex and long-drawn-out series of manoeuvres attended the attempt to obtain an act for Fordington, and in this case the promoters were eventually obliged to admit defeat. The initial proposal appears to have come from the lord of the manor, the Duchy of Cornwall, in 1801 but, according to Endacott, the scheme was voted down by the tenants (Endacott, 1938, p. 32). Certainly the bill which Parliament had agreed to consider was, in the technical phrase, 'not brought in' in the 1802-3 session (CJ 58/147). The scheme was revived in 1808, using the advice of a highly experienced enclosure commissioner, Thomas Davis of Horningsham. Davis drew up the bill but this had to be dropped when it was realised that the majority in favour was far too small even if those declaring themselves neutral were included, as Parliament was sometimes prepared to accept. A further attempt in 1812 also foundered. Endacott records that the tithe lessee, William Morton Pitt, took a leading role for the opposition, amongst his stated objections being the opposition of most of the farmers and of the inhabitants of Dorchester, which he clearly felt should not be ignored whatever the legal situation

(Endacott, pp. 36 and 41-42). However, this is at odds with the evidence of a letter of 8 October 1813, which places Pitt in the opposite camp, and gives a Mr Charles Mitchell as the organiser of the opposition. Mitchell was trying to persuade the tenants that they could enclose without the expense of an act.[21] Another letter, from Davis, describes the opponents merely as certain attorneys in Dorchester and advocates circulating the bill privately, rather than holding a public meeting, since he clearly feared that the size and vehemence of the opposition would sway or frighten waverers.

All these efforts proved abortive. No bill was passed, and Mitchell's scheme for an enclosure by agreement also failed, leaving the whole system nominally intact. Endacott records that nothing was done until 1876, when the customary tenants were bought out, giving the lord a free hand to reorganise at his leisure (Endacott, p. 43). However, there is an agreement recorded in the manorial court minutes for 1841 to divide the West Fields into two sections, to be enclosed in alternate years, the enclosed half to be cropped as the occupier wished.[22] While this was not technically an enclosure as normally defined, it was a type of 'halfway house' which may have allowed the outward appearance of the system to survive for a further 35 years, while giving the farmers a measure of flexibility.

Disputes over who did, or did not, have a legal claim to rights on commons are to be expected, since many manors made little attempt to pursue minor infringements and many genuine right-owners had no written support for their claims. More surprising were some of the other disputes which arose. At Chesilbourne, for example, a wrangle developed over whether a piece of land was freehold or, as R.R. Harvey, agent to Lord Rivers, alleged, leased from the Rivers estate under a lease of 1795.

One curiosity of the procedures in Dorset was the power given in several acts for the proprietors to appoint 'quality men'. These individuals were commonly used in one or two midland counties to value the lands to be enclosed, but their use elsewhere was unusual, since this was regarded as one of the duties of the commissioners. The reasons why such powers were written into Dorset acts is unclear, particularly as they occur in the nineteenth century, for example at Winterbourne Abbas in 1808, by which time they had become even less of a normal feature nationally. Since acts were frequently copied from earlier ones, it is possible that some agent used a midlands example as his model, and that this in turn became the model for many more; equally, it may have been that some individuals decided, for purely local reasons, that quality men were a good idea. In practice there is little evidence that the powers were normally exercised, and the commissioners, or one of them, normally took on this responsibility.

The fact that William Jennings, the sole commissioner at Plush, deputed the job of valuing the land to someone else actually became the subject of an appeal. Charles Sturt and Leonard Pount took a case to the quarter sessions, citing this as one of their grounds for complaint, and accusing Jennings of partiality in his award, maintaining that the allotment made in the open fields did not include adequate compensation for the rights lost on the down. The court clearly accepted that while the commissioner had ultimate responsibility he did not have to do everything personally, and they judged Jennings' award fair. The case was therefore thrown out.[23]

The impression is sometimes given that appeals against the commissioners' judgements were impossible, but another case demonstrates that this was not so. Thomas Abbott successfully appealed against Thomas Davis's award for Winterbourne Monkton on the grounds that he had made an error in this particular allotment. Unfortunately the precise nature of the problem is not recorded in the judgement, but not only was Abbott given substantial monetary compensation, Davis was obliged to pay the costs.[24] Fear of such an action may well explain why commissioners often chose to allocate a block in each former field or common to an individual, rather than one single block in one particular area, since the latter was far more likely to raise disputes over their valuations.

Formal Agreements

The task of determining precisely how many formal agreements were reached in Dorset is no easy one, let alone providing any exact figure for acreages. There were a number of bilateral agreements to exchange land, for example at Seaborough,[25] and it is often by no means clear from the surviving documentation whether these represent the formal abolition of open fields or commons, or were merely a private arrangement to improve the layout of particular estates. The fact that a series of such arrangements, possibly over a long period of time, might ultimately result in the loss of a complete system merely serves to complicate the unravelling of the story. Such a long-drawn-out case can surely only be regarded as piecemeal, in contrast to the sudden sweeping away of a whole system as occurred, for example at Buckland Newton. It is not always clear whether authors such as Taylor are using the same definition of 'enclosure by agreement' as that adopted here. Some agreements are dubious for other reasons. Bloxworth was an agreement for afforestation of part of the commons, carried out under the act of 29 George II, and there is a case for omitting it.

Additionally, Dorset agreements suffer from all the vagaries of presentation outlined in Chapter 3. Both the agreements for Milborne St Andrew, for example, contain acreages for part of the land only; the earlier, for Milborne and Roak Downs specifies the allotments to each owner merely in terms of points of the compass, while the second, discussed in more detail below, does the same for the largest owner, specifying acreages only for the subdivision of the remainder amongst the other owners. Only 11 post-1700 agreements have either a complete award or detailed figures in the agreement, so it is not possible to be as precise about the outcome as one might wish.

Bearing this in mind, it is nevertheless obvious that, as is characteristic of most of the country, formal agreements played a relatively small part in the enclosure history of Dorset, or even in the non-parliamentary part (see fig. 9). Thirty-eight formal agreements have been discovered, and of these eighteen fell before 1700, and are thus strictly speaking outside the scope of this study. No less than seven, however, belong to the 1690s, and thus lead directly into the period under consideration, and there might be a case for including them in the analysis. Prior to 1690 there had been a break of almost 70 years since the West Parley agreement of 1633,[26] and there appears to have been an upsurge of interest in

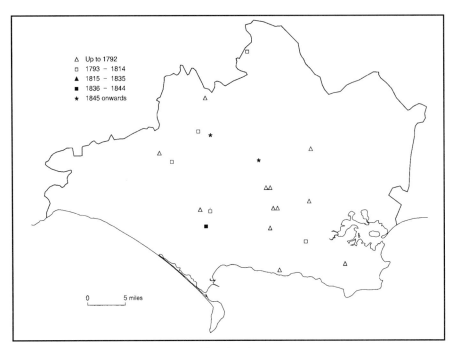

9. Location and timing of formal enclosure agreements in Dorset.

enclosure in the last decade of the seventeenth century. If these are included, the total becomes 27, rather than 20.

Dorset is not untypical in that, although agreements were being concluded well before the main period of enclosure by act, they were not replaced by them. Formal agreements continued well into the middle of the nineteenth century (see fig. 4.6), and the last, that for Hilton, dates from 1855, almost at the end of the parliamentary period. What is, perhaps, surprising, given the very small numbers involved, is the continuity of the temporal pattern, and the fact that the few breaks in the pattern are precisely where one would expect them.

The later agreements for which figures can be produced tended to be concerned with a relatively small acreage. While two from the seventeenth century involved over a thousand acres, 1300 at Stour Prevost and 1605 at West Parley, only Holnest, of the rest, exceeded 300 acres. At the other extreme only Hilton, at 28 acres, fell below 100.[27] They thus dealt individually with far less land than the average Dorset parliamentary enclosure, though most were substantially above the small enclosures frequent under the 1845 act.

Part of the reason for this is that later Dorset agreements tended to deal with field or common separately, rather than whole systems. In the 1690s, both Buckland Newton (1699) and Abbotsbury (1692) involved a mixture of field, meadow, common, and down, though unfortunately the acreages concerned have not survived. The Cerne Abbas agreement of 1795 also seems to have been more comprehensive, with field, common and down, but unfortunately no award could be discovered to confirm the precise details. The only other later one with an apparently comprehensive cover, Affpuddle in 1743, records a mere 158 acres, a highly misleading figure since, though the agreement makes provision for exchanges of common meadow and field, the award lists only the allotments on the common. More usually, agreements concentrated on one or two items. The Fordington agreement of 1841 seems to have been solely concerned with the fields, while Moreton (1744), and Rushton (1813) were purely for commons, and Evershot (1785) and Frome St Quinton (1805) for hill or down.

An extreme example of this tendency to deal with areas separately is actually an early one, provided by the parish of Morden. This had three separate agreements in the two years 1694 and 1695. Two covered the open fields of West Morden and East Morden respectively, while the third covered only Morden Meadow. The logic of this was, no doubt, that a different mix of individuals had holdings in the three areas, and that it was therefore simpler to conclude a specific agreement with each group, rather than trying to create one single one which might have run into difficulties. The first two were between the lord, Thomas Erle of Charbarrow, and the freeholders within each of the respective manors, whereas the third included both freeholders and tenants, and was specifically stated to be at the request of the latter, who wished to 'discontinue their tenantry in common in the said meadow'.[28]

What is worthy of note about the Dorset agreements is the degree to which they were concerned with common and waste. While in the other counties agreements were used proportionately more to enclose open field, and acts for common, in Dorset this is reversed (see fig. 10). Though the inadequate documentation makes the details rather suspect, there is little doubt that the broad picture is correct. Dorset, for reasons which remain obscure, used the two methods in a markedly different way.

The advantages to the small owners of enclosing by agreement can be seen at Abbotsbury. Not only did they avoid the expenses inevitable in obtaining an act, but Thomas Strangeways, the main driving force behind the scheme, paid all the costs. Had they gone to an act, as they might well have done 60 years later, not only would they all have had to pay a share, but the total bill would almost certainly have been greater. This was undoubtedly used as a means of exerting pressure on owners to conclude an agreement; the threat of an expensive and long-drawn-out parliamentary procedure could often persuade any waverers. On the other hand, as the Fordington wrangle shows, this could work in reverse, with those favouring an agreement working to stymie a bill, and in that case producing a stalemate.

The arrangements for formal agreements show a similar range of idiosyncrasies to those of the acts, though in this case unfettered by parliamentary scrutiny. The Affpuddle agreement specified that the new owners were to grub up any timber so that James Frampton, the lord, could remove it. The separate Affpuddle Heath agreement stated that all parties would put their allotments to tillage within 14 months of enclosing them. At Evershot, the number of sheep pasture rights owed by an individual were to be used to determine his or her share in the common; at Hilfield, on the other hand, the proportion of the poor rate paid by each claimant was to be used. It is not clear why this method was chosen at Hilfield, though it may be that the common there was

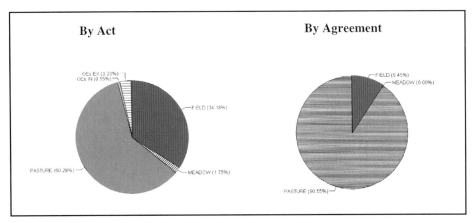

10. *Comparison of types of land affected by enclosure acts (left) and agreements in Dorset.*

unstinted, or that there was some dispute over the stints, and that the poor rate seemed the most appropriate measure to avoid any disputes.

The problems which might arise with agreements are well illustrated by the case of Milborne St Andrew. According to documents held in the Dorset Record Office,[29] John Cole, lord of the manor of Milborne St Andrew, reached an agreement with Edmund Morton Pleydell, lord of the adjoining manor of Milborne Churchstone, and William Biles, a local yeoman, allowing Cole to enclose land called Stablebarrow and Ingores. Pleydell's tenants objected, and in 1749, some five years after the original agreement, Pleydell took the case to the Court of Chancery, alleging that he was 'unwarily drawn in to sign a deed of exchange' on assurances from Cole and Biles that the other tenants had no common rights on these lands. There appear to have been other niggling disputes between the parties, for example over Cole's attempt to restrict access to Outgore before May, rather than 10th March as the tenants claimed was the custom, and over the turning out of cattle into growing corn.

The end result was a formal agreement drawn up in November 1749 and implemented the following year. By its terms, Cole got the common fields called Ingore, Stablebarrow and Outgore and all of North Field north of Green Way. Coles in exchange gave up any claim to Lynes, Brooklands Field, the southern part of North Field, and just over 18 acres of Great Field, all of which were to be divided and enclosed by the other parties. Three referees were appointed to oversee the division, and were given powers akin to those normal for parliamentary commissioners, such as the right to create roads, and to order fences and hedges.

Informal Enclosure

As has already been discussed, informal enclosures, by their very nature, are not susceptible to the sort of analysis carried out on the other two methods. While it is easy to count the number of acts or agreements, to assign a date to them, and to attempt a calculation of the amount of land involved, there is no possibility of doing so with any precision for the informal enclosures. Apart from any other consideration, informal piecemeal enclosure undoubtedly affected many of the parishes covered by formal procedures, and it was sometimes only when the possibilities of this means had been exhausted that formal methods were used to tidy up the remains. It is also probable that in some instances informal piecemeal enclosure was directly responsible for formal action, in that it so reduced the field or common that it became unworkable.

A minimum indication of the scale of informal enclosures can be derived from the Enclosure Index.[30] From this, it would seem that exactly one third (39) of the 117 field systems mentioned as operating in 1700 were enclosed *entirely* by informal methods; of the 40 known common meadows, 21 vanished in this way, and 35 parishes lost all their commons. However, there is ample indication of other informal enclosure, often on a considerable scale. Holnest common was finally enclosed by agreement in 1799, but over the preceeding 16 years at least 50 acres, over 7 per cent of the total, had been encroached by the lord;[31] Hooke down survived as common until at least 1841, but has a recorded history of encroachments from 1733 onwards.[32] At Bere Regis, 70 acres are recorded as taken from the down in 1773, and a Mr Turberville had been taking land from both the open fields and the commons and downs over a century and a half earlier, yet parts of both the fields and the commons survived to be finally enclosed under a General Act in 1846. Similarly, the various parts of the commons in East Stoke and Rushton were subject to an enclosure agreement of 1813 and an enclosure by parliamentary order completed in 1870, but encroachments continued from the mid eighteenth century into the late nineteenth.[33] A heavily annotated survey of 1811 records, for example, the exchange of seven pieces in Rushton Meadow for land in Rushton Stockford and Binegar, and the receipt of 14 acres of common field in exchange for 3.75 acres of land elsewhere.[34]

The temporal pattern of informal enclosures can only be sketched in, at best. What is very clear, however, is that it was not just a feature of the early eighteenth century. Fourteen of the lost common field systems survived into the nineteenth as did 6 of the common meadows, and at least 12 parishes had commons in 1800 but lost them by 1900. Nor were the later survivals necessarily small, as has sometimes been argued. The abortive bill for Fordington records 3500 acres as being open in 1814.

A typical example of the sort of process operating is provided by Nether Compton. 158 acres were already enclosed by the early eighteenth century, but a lease of 1800 specifically refers to an acre 'in the common fields called Brimpton Field' and two acres in Clanfield common field. By the time of the tithe survey of 1838, remnants of Brympton, Clanfield, Uppingstock, Cary Hill, West and Ridgeway Fields can still be identified; they were still in unfenced strips with scattered ownership, and the tithe surveyor describes them as 'in' a particular field, a description characteristic of open fields. The total area, however, was only 19.34 acres. Both Brimpton Field and Clanfield were still nominally open and common in 1854, and finally disappeared when properties were exchanged in 1863 under the General Act for Enclosure and Exchange.[35] It is highly unlikely that they were still genuinely common by the mid-nineteenth century, but they were certainly open in part, and the ownership pattern was still intermixed. The stumbling block in this case may well have been that one of the owners was the Bradford Abbas and Clifton Maybank Charity School, and doubts about the powers of the trustees to enter into a legally binding agreement delayed any final reorganisation until the general act cleared the way.

Leases and surveys of the manors of Stoborough, Arne and Sleap illustrate the gradual nature of the process. A lease of 1753 refers to 'a certain parcel of Common Heath… as it was formerly allotted and bounded out', (implying a formal agreement, though none has been found), and a lease of 1764 similarly mentions five acres 'in the Common Fields there now inclosed' and to 'now inclosed' waste. However, the 1753 lease also records pasture rights in the heath, showing that some remained, and references to foreshares in Arne Common Meadow and to rights in Slepe Moor persist until 1772, though encroachments on the latter occur in 1764. Suddenly, in 1790, the word 'common' disappears from Arne Meadow, as do mentions of foreshares, indicating an abandonment of communal practices during the late 1770s or the 1780s. In other words, it appears that the various elements of the communal system were demolished individually over a period of at least thirty years.

Dorset had a number of examples of lords of the manor waiting patiently for copyholds or leases to end, consolidating piecemeal whenever the opportunity offered and withdrawing land from communal use once all the rights in a particular area had fallen into their hands. 'Mr Webb', apparently one of the well-known family of land agents and enclosure commissioners, ended a survey of the Horton Estate in 1791 by pointing out that the 800 acres of The Heath 'is not set at any value in the foregoing calculation' but that, once the lifeholds fell in, it would form an ideal area for timber planting, with an estimated income of £50,000 in 100 years' time.[36] A similar situation was envisaged at Piddletrenthide, where a survey of 1771 points out that Winchester College were the sole owners of 1,091 acres of various downlands which would prove very profitable if enclosed, 'but such an enclosure cannot be made until the several copies fall into hand either by death or purchase'.[37] In this particular case patience apparently ran out, since the process was cut short by an act of 1815.

Summary

The final challenge is clearly to try to give some assessment of the relative importance of the various processes within Dorset. All the evidence which could be gathered suggests that parliamentary enclosure was the dominant process in the county after 1700, but not by any great amount. If the parliamentary total is set at just over 103,000 acres, or almost $16\frac{1}{2}$ per cent of the county area, then the overall total for the two centuries seems to have been of the order of 190,000 acres, or just over 30 per cent. In this respect, as in so many other aspects of its enclosure, Dorset falls between Hampshire and Sussex, with their greater reliance on non-parliamentary means, and Wiltshire, with its bias towards the act.

5

Hampshire

Hampshire is the largest of the counties under consideration, and shows great variation in its agricultural potential even today. In the eighteenth century these contrasts were much sharper. The chalklands of the central and north-western parts of the county, traditionally difficult land for the farmer to handle, were being reappraised as a result of changing techniques, and were being rapidly upgraded in the eyes, and more specifically the expectations, of local landowners. At the opposite extreme, extensive areas of the east and north-east of the county consisted of poor sandy and gravely soils covered by heath and scrub, land in which only the most hopelessly optimistic saw any possible agricultural potential. The extreme example of this was the New Forest, forming a major block of heath and woodland towards the south-west, though it must be appreciated that in 1700 several similar forests still existed, for example Bere and Woolmer. In the south of the county, the coastal plain and the south-facing slopes of the chalk were traditionally some of the finest agricultural land, but they were facing both major opportunities and major threats from the growing urban areas. Around Portsmouth, for example, the communal agricultural systems were crumbling under the twin influences of, on the one hand, the market for fresh vegetables and, on the other, the physical encroachment of the built-up area (see Chapman, 1978).

The distribution of open field systems in the county closely reflects this pattern. As can be seen from fig. 11, they were widespread throughout the chalklands of the centre and north of the county, with a noticeable line down the Avon valley in the west, and a cluster in the south-eastern coastal area. Apart from the New Forest, the main gaps lay in the sandy lands of the east of the county, and in the agriculturally similar strip in the extreme north.

Of the common arable systems that the authors have been able to identify in the county, it would appear that only 39 were fully enclosed before 1700.[1] Still operative were 196, at least in part, in 1700, and a total of 65 was still in existence as late as 1800. Nineteen of these apparently remained open when the tithe surveys for their parishes were made. Open field enclosure, at least after 1700, was thus primarily a feature of the eighteenth century: almost 67 per cent of the final enclosures occurred then, as opposed to only 33 per cent in the century which followed. A number of parishes possessed several separate systems. Two systems were not unusual, while two parishes

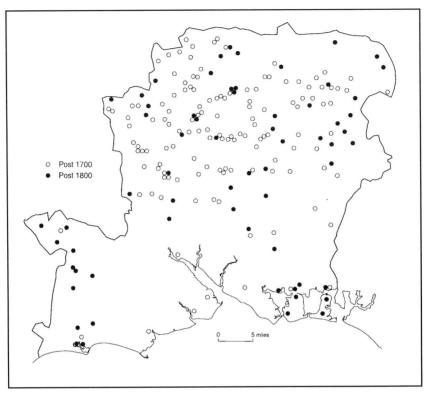

11. Localities with surviving open fields in Hampshire in 1700 and 1800.

had three systems, five had four, and four had five systems. Of the remaining parishes where no systems have been traced, many in the heathy areas probably never had open fields, though there are occasional suggestions of very early enclosures. Hampshire also lost some villages, and no doubt the systems which went with them, during the major period of desertions in the later Middle Ages (see Beresford and Hurst, 1971).

The distribution of commons and wastes shows a significant contrast to that of the fields. While almost all parishes with open field still retained their commons in 1700, a great many of those which lacked fields nevertheless had commons, often of great extent. One of the attractions of the heathlands, to which mention has already been made, was the existence of extensive areas of common grazing, which offered a livelihood even to smallholders. The royal forests themselves, restrictive though their regulations were, were subject to common grazing rights, which were of great value to those fortunate enough to be able to claim them; indeed, it is above all in the New Forest, within the area of this study, where such rights continue to be exercised today.

Bearing in mind the usual cautions about precision, at least 240 systems of commons were in operation in 1700, and 196 of these were still present in 1800. According to Hoskins and Stamp (1963), 41 remained at the time of their survey. In crude terms, therefore, some 17 per cent of 'townships' retain some common, though normally in extremely attenuated form, while 18 per cent lost theirs during the eighteenth century. For the remainder, almost 65 per cent, commons were finally abolished between 1800 and 1900.

Common meadows were somewhat less numerous, relatively, in Hampshire than in Dorset or Wiltshire, though they were locally of considerable significance to the communities involved, and were occasionally of considerable size. Given the varied physical background of the county, it is scarcely surprising that their distribution was uneven, for rivers suitable for the traditional wet meadows of the southern counties are lacking in much of the east. In the Avon Valley and in parts of the chalklands, on the other hand, ideal situations existed, and common meadows formed a vital part of the agricultural economy.

Seventy-one 'townships' contained common meadow in 1700, and 44 of these persisted until at least 1800. Hoskins and Stamp record one, Droxford, as still retaining common meadow in their survey in the mid-twentieth century. As with the commons, therefore, over 60 per cent of the townships lost their meadows in the nineteenth century.

The Background to Enclosure

The enclosure pattern in Hampshire might be described as something of a 'mixed bag', reflecting the diversity of both the physical and human geography of the county. As has already been suggested, the large areas of sandy, heathy soils offered no real incentive for early enclosure. Under eighteenth century conditions they would support little other than poor quality pasture, and it was not until the later nineteenth century, in general, that urban demands and the beginnings of widespread conifer planting offered viable alternatives. Though squatters and individual farmers might feel the need to make small encroachments for their own specific purposes, there was no general pressure to replace these large tracts of woodland and open pasture with a network of small individual properties, which would have been less useful for grazing animals and more costly to maintain. The fact that several of the main areas of waste were subject to *intercommoning* (the sharing of grazing rights between several manors) and that crown rights were involved in the Forests, meant that the use of the expensive parliamentary method of enclosure was almost inevitable. It is therefore hardly surprising that the balance of waste enclosure was so heavily towards the nineteenth century, and that a significant amount awaited the much cheaper procedures under the General Act of 1845.

The chalklands were a different matter. Most parishes there had some common arable, and the balance between this and the waste was far better than in some of the Midland counties. There was thus no desperate need to enclose in order to convert the common arable to pasture, as seems to have been the case in parts of the Midlands, but new techniques of managing the chalk offered incentives. The sheep-and-corn husbandry which had long been characteristic of this area of the county had been

12. Studland Heath. A lowland heath, typical of many Dorset commons prior to enclosure.

subject to gradual change, and by 1700 the introduction of clover, sainfoin, ryegrass and turnips was beginning to meet the perennial problem of stock feeding over the winter months. However, such crops were difficult to incorporate into a fully functional common field system, and abolishing it would greatly simplify their use.

There was a further problem with the traditional arrangements. The classic open field system implied a rigid and unchanging division between arable, meadow and pasture, and such a fixed pattern was peculiarly unsuited to the chalklands, where fertility was liable to a steady decline under continuous cropping. Many parts of England had, of necessity, adopted more flexible variants, with temporary grass leys within the fields and temporary 'brecks' from the common waste, and the Hampshire chalklands were no exception. Nevertheless, they were too close to the textbook model to avoid the problems. For the larger farmer, at least, the total flexibility of land in severalty offered a prospect both of higher profits and of maintaining the land in better heart.

The patterns of both landownership and tenancy within the chalklands tended to favour agricultural innovation, and hence early enclosure. Many landowners had large estates here, and were theoretically in a position to experiment with agricultural innovations, using knowledge acquired either by osmosis from landowners in neighbouring areas and counties, or from their estates in other parts of the country where new techniques had already proved valuable. However, in contrast to Sussex, large parts of these estates were still entangled within communal systems, which made experimentation difficult and the widespread application of new techniques even more so. Enclosure seemed the key to both agricultural advance and greater profit.

The tenancy situation led to the same conclusion. This region was well-suited to large farms, and such units were becoming common there by the eighteenth century (Jones, 1958): by 1794, most farms in this area lay in the rent-range £200 to £300 per annum, and a farm in the latter category might typically consist of 400 acres of arable, 100 acres of down and 30 acres of water meadow (Vancouver, 1810). However, tenants with the necessary capital resources to take advantage of such large enterprises would almost certainly be interested in further agricultural innovation in order to obtain a good return on their investment. They needed to be able to farm grain on a large scale, using flexible rotations of grain, grass and clover ley, and to lay the land to grass when production was exhausted. Enclosure was the key to this flexibility, and a landowner seeking progressive, commercially minded tenants willing to pay high rents had to bear this in mind.

A further factor was the changing local legal framework. By about 1700, the firm control which many Hampshire manors had apparently previously exercised over the system of husbandry had often lapsed. The remaining post-1700 court books concentrate mainly on changes of tenant and presentments for non-payment of rent and encroachments on the waste, and both these and the estate maps, which were produced sporadically, indicate widespread consolidation and engrossment. As a consequence, in many parishes, common arable systems were in a state of decay by the later eighteenth century, and were therefore ripe for final full enclosure.

The formal agreement offered a ready means of achieving the desired effect, and was often adopted in Hampshire. An early example is to be found in the north-western chalklands, at Amport, and they continued to be used to enclose substantial acreages in the middle to late eighteenth century. For example, 473.56 acres were enclosed at Brown Candover in 1737; 1,598.96 acres at Goodworth Clatford in 1777; 1,182.75 acres at Brown Candover and Northington in 1792.[2] Common arable was always an easier target for enclosers, since tenancy patterns were much more clear-cut and improved rentals tended to follow swiftly, so it is no surprise that open fields formed a substantial part of the land involved.

Much of the rest of the enclosure came about through various informal methods, which, as always, have left behind very little documentary evidence. However, Hampshire is relatively well blessed with estate maps, surveys, rentals and particulars, and the documentation arising from the Tithe Commutation Act of 1836 is of particular help in identifying some of the 'lost' systems.

Such informal enclosure continued to accompany both of the more formal methods, and it is not uncommon to find parishes with more than one parliamentary enclosure or with a parliamentary enclosure and an agreement enclosure, or even with clear signs of all three methods.[3] In this respect, Hampshire shows significant differences from the Midlands, where most commonable land in many parishes seems to have been enclosed at a stroke by a single Act of Parliament. In much of Hampshire, very few common husbandry systems were running in their pure state by the time that enclosure was in its stride. Most exhibited a mixture of strips separated purely by baulks in a sometimes bleak hedgeless landscape, being tilled on a communal basis, juxtaposed with narrow, hedged fields enclosed straight out of the engrossed and consolidated strips.

It should also be noted that Hampshire provides clear evidence that enclosure did not necessarily have to be imposed on an unwilling tenantry from above.

Often, tenants wanted to enclose but were prevented from doing so by their lords, as at Wootton St. Lawrence in the early seventeenth century, when the tenants made suit to Sir William Uvedale for one to be carried out. Far from leaping at the opportunity, Uvedale refused, and demanded £40 for his consent, which effectively deterred them from pursuing the matter further. In the same parish, the tenants of Manydown manor, who had succeeded in having their land enclosed, rapidly retreated from a dispute when a threat was made to throw it open again (see pp. 84-5).

Parliamentary Enclosures

Full details of all Hampshire's parliamentary enclosures are contained in the authors' *A Guide to Enclosures in Hampshire*, and information on individual acts and awards may be sought there. All told, there were 161 parliamentary enclosures which fell wholly or largely within the historic county, plus the act which covered the open fields of Warblington parish, but which also dealt with several systems in Sussex. This latter is indexed under Sussex (number 36014) in the National Enclosure Project, but the part relating to Warblington has been included in the acreages for Hampshire. The Portsea act of 1753, which is included in many lists, has been omitted, since the 'Portsea Common' to which it refers was not by that stage any longer a common. It was merely a district of the town, and the arrangements detailed in the act do not, in fact, constitute an enclosure.

For those enclosures where an award exists (including awards confirmed by a later act), each individual allotment was totalled; for the remaining eight various other sources were used. Four have a figure given in the act and, whatever doubts there may be about its accuracy, this has been used. For the other four an estimate has been included based on such local details as could be found. These last are unlikely to be highly accurate, but are likely to be of the right order of magnitude. The one major problem is the case of St Mary Bourne, where an act of 1815 supposedly confirmed an agreement of 1772, covering 2,537 acres. However, the act makes clear that it applied only to the allotments made to Elizabeth and John Carter, which together amounted to a mere 116 acres, and its purpose was more to clarify family arrangements than to enclose anything. If the whole of the 2,537 acres is included, then parliamentary enclosure accounted for 139,426 acres, while if it is totally omitted the figure falls to 136,889. These figures compare with Turner's total of 156,522 (Turner, 1980, p. 178). The discrepancy appears to arise from Turner's method of accounting for missing figures, since in the case of Hampshire the missing enclosures are in fact significantly smaller than the mean.

In terms of the type of land involved, precision is limited by that part of the acreage which cannot be accurately assigned, amounting to some 7.8 per cent of the total. However, the overall balance is clear. Over 64 per cent of the land was common and waste, over 28 per cent open field, and just under 1.3 per cent common meadow. Even

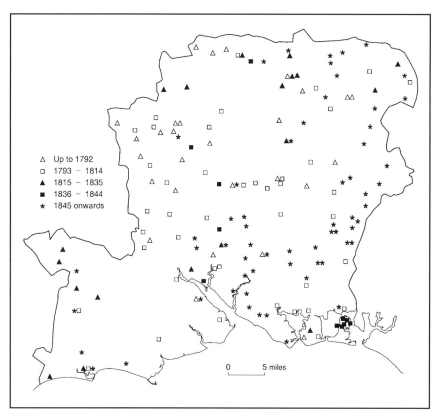

13. Location and timing of Hampshire parliamentary enclosures.

if we take only the eighteenth century part of the movement, common and waste dominated, though only by 55.5 per cent against just under 39. Parliamentary enclosure in the county was thus overwhelmingly concerned with bringing new land into cultivation, rather than consolidating holdings in the open fields.

As has already been noted, there is a marked spatial and temporal pattern to the parliamentary movement within the county. Its origins are in the central chalklands, especially those adjoining the Wiltshire border, in the north-west. From there it spread through the rest of the chalklands during the period of the Napoleonic Wars, with a final late burst of activity in the south and east after the passing of the 1845 General Act (see fig 13 above). Temporally, there is a contrast, as is not unusual in other counties, between the maximum number of individual enclosures, and the peak acreage. The former falls clearly in the 1850s, but many of these were relatively small in area, and the peak acreage was actually in the decade of the 1810s (compare figs. 14 and 15).

These enclosures are now, to us, accomplished facts, but the documents that record their creation hide the, often complicated, negotiations that were necessary to reach the required level of agreement before it was worth presenting a bill to Parliament. Correspondence of 1792[4] between the parties to the enclosure of Basing draws attention

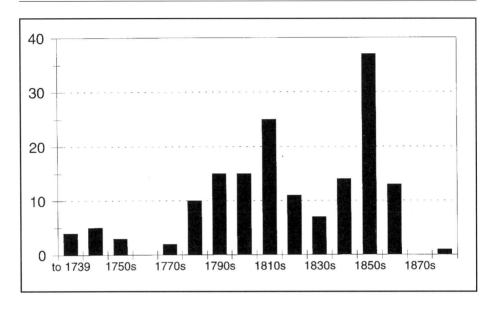

Figs. 14 & 15. Timing of Hampshire enclosure acts and orders by decade (above), and acreages enclosed in Hampshire by act or order in each decade.

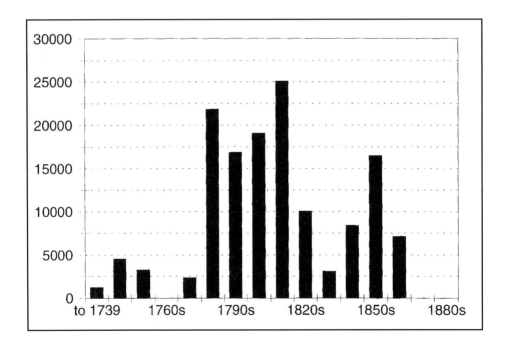

to the objections of Mr. John Limbrey, who was ultimately the recipient of the second largest allotment in the final award. William Bishop wrote to Lord Bolton that Mr. Sclater (another proprietor) had been enjoined by Mr. Limbrey not only to oppose it in his (Mr. Limbrey's) name, but to strengthen the opposition 'by resorting to you and all possible Parliamentary interest'. Mr. Limbrey was at this time [December 1792] dangerously ill, so the meeting was adjourned to the 17th January, it being decided that

> if the event much apprehended should happen to Mr. Limbrey in the mean time, the measure might yet proceed, especially as there appears scarcely another dissenting voice.

The enclosure had originally been intended to cover both Basing and land in the neighbouring parish of Upton Grey, but the delay arising from Mr. Limbrey's objection led to the Upton Grey proprietors initiating a Bill of their own, the award for which was completed in 1796.[5] The parties at Basing were keen that the bill should not be delayed to a later session of Parliament, and so Bishop suggested they proceed on the assumption that Mr. Limbrey would succumb to his affliction, thus allowing the measure to go ahead. In a letter of the 8th January 1793,[6] Bishop characterised the dissent of Mr. Limbrey

> [as] both sudden and unexpected… for he had previously signified both to [Bishop] and to his tenants his hearty acquiescence.

In fact, agreement had seemed so likely that the tenants had begun to alter the mode of culture of the fields in preparation for the completion of the enclosure and 'this would by the Bill's procrastination… rather injuriously affect them than otherwise'. In Bishop's view, Limbrey's sudden change of mind arose from his experience of an earlier enclosure, since he had commented that 'he was used ill in the Basingstoke Inclosure'. No doubt to the consternation of the others, Limbrey recovered from his life-threatening illness, placing the whole scheme in jeopardy. The correspondence does not reveal how agreement was finally achieved, but Basing was eventually enclosed by act of 1796, with the final award in 1797.

Hampshire, like the other counties, had its share of failed bills, and also a number of proposed enclosures which never even reached Parliament. In the case of Bransbury (alias Bramsbury) Common in Barton Stacey, there is evidence as to why a proposal failed to progress. In the Winchester Cathedral Archives[7] are the comments of one Philip Williams, advising the Dean and Chapter on the draft bill presented for their approval. Williams raised a number of objections, for example to the clause allowing land to be sold to raise the costs of the enclosure, but his principal concern was the clause entitling Sir Henry Wilson to the right of the soil by virtue of his lordship of Barton Stacey manor. Bransbury was a separate manor, the lords of which were the Dean and Chapter, and Williams could find no evidence that it was subordinate to Barton Stacey. He therefore recommended that 'I cannot advise the Dean and Chapter on any account to give their consent to the bill, as long as that objectionable clause remains in it'. The bill was never sent to Parliament, and Bransbury Common is still unenclosed.

An enclosure act might sometimes be used as the means of bringing to an end a long history of argument and legal wrangling. The 826.48 acres of common which were enclosed at Hurstbourne Tarrant in 1820[8] had been a source of trouble over a very long period. The area covered by the enclosure consisted of Doles Wood and Grubbed Grounds, which had been the subject of a lawsuit in the time of James I, *c.* 1620, over allegations by the lord that the commoners 'had made several inclosures every man a close', and were trying to enlarge their rights of common of pasture.[9] Disputes continued, with the commoners claiming that the lord was cutting the wood 'out of course', and a series of verdicts at common law, confirmed in the Court of Chancery, established that of the twelve coppices which made up the area, the lord could enclose four at any one time, leaving eight open for the commoners. The lord could fell a coppice every second year, but the eight left open must be of at least eight years' growth. In 1771 there was a further dispute, with the commoners alleging malpractice on the part of the lord and his tenants.[10] Part of the coppice was recorded as 'lately being cleard of wood, and is now pasture grounds', the cleared area having acquired the name 'Grubb Lands'. The commoners had been refused entry to the Grubb Lands when they should have reverted to common, and the lord's tenant was felling wood at too young a stage of its development. They agreed to appoint Mr John Todd, an Andover attorney, to prosecute the case for them. The parliamentary enclosure of 1820 therefore put an end to at least two centuries of wrangling over the coppices. It did not, however, put an end to common rights, for some 200 acres were left open for the commoners' use. These remained until 1852, when the rights were abolished in exchange for £250, which was to be invested for the general benefit and welfare of the parish.

Parliamentary enclosure was a costly procedure, and various means were employed to cover the expenses incurred. During the preparations for the Hursley enclosure, carried out between 1809 and 1813, Sir William Heathcote, the major landowner, paid a total of £1,000 to the bankers, for which sum he was allowed interest of five percent until it was repaid.[11] In effect, he was subsidising the process, and continued to do so throughout. In March 1810, Sir William advanced a further sum of £1,000, against which expenditure of £1,183 4s. 7d. was paid to the commissioners, surveyors and clerk. Of the total costs for the Hursley enclosure of £4,617 5s. 5d., Heathcote paid a share of £3,352 13s. 8d., reflecting the fact that he received 80.77 per cent or 1830 acres of the total of 2,567 acres enclosed. When charges like these were taken into account, it is understandable that proprietors often felt that it would not be profitable to enclose small areas of common or waste by act. Such thinking accounts for the exclusion of $23\frac{1}{2}$ acres of Whitsbury Common from the enclosure there of 1802.[12]

The legal status of the land to be enclosed had to be determined at the outset. Illegal encroachments (normally, in Hampshire, those made within twenty-one years of the proposed enclosure) were held to be a part of the commonable land. All proprietors had to submit claims against their own holdings, and this led to disputes at times, if not objections. The chief land owner at the enclosure of Hursley in 1809, Sir William

Heathcote, objected to 16 of the 31 claims received, and it was the task of the commissioners to hear evidence and satisfy themselves that the claims they ultimately considered for the enclosure were good ones. Those claiming allotments often asked the commissioners to give them allotments in particular locations to provide compactness of holding. Indeed, at the Forest of Bere enclosure the commissioners advertised in a local paper, inviting all those whose claims had been accepted to write 'as to the situation of their intended allotments'.[13] Commissioners did their best to comply with these wishes, but consolidation might sometimes only be achieved through an active process of exchanges, particularly of old enclosures, although enclosure allotments were also involved. The quantities of land exchanged are often not matched in terms of acreage, but this reflected the type of land and its quality, and must have offered compensation for the convenience of having parcels of land laid together.

Precisely how many of the parties did make specific requests is not easy to determine, though presumably the larger and more literate landowners were the most likely to respond. At the enclosure of Broughton in 1790 twenty seven manorial tenants lodged claims, and four individuals appear to have made particular requests about the location of their lands. One of the major holders, Mrs. Steele, received her allotments placed together near her three farms called Pigeon House, Godfreys and Goddards, and it was stated that if there were to be sufficient land to take the rest of her allotment out of the Down, that was to be allotted at the extremity of the parish. Another landowner, Robert Thistlethwayte wished to have his allotments as near as possible to his newly refurbished buildings. If this was not feasible, he would be content to have his allotments laid into one, which was what happened, the resulting holding being called Lords Farm. A tenant with a smaller holding of one acre in Green Hedge Field, one Richard Rogis, asked for 8 acres to allocated adjoining, and James King of Gosport requested one yardland to be allotted near 'home', though it was not specified where that was.

In many cases, a great deal of the wrangling took place before a bill was presented, and some degree of accommodation had to be reached if the bill were to succeed. This is well illustrated from the extensive papers which have survived concerning the enclosure of the Forest of Bere in 1814. Previous attempts to enclose the Forest had got as far as abortive bills in 1801 and 1801-2,[14] but all had failed, amongst other reasons, through the lack of support from Thomas Thistlethwayte, Hereditary Warden of the Forest and lord of the manor, who felt that they did not 'deal adequately with the encroachments and depredations that were committed on all parts of the forest'.[15]

Thistlethwayte had other concerns about the new Bill. It had been proposed that 500 acres should go to the Crown and 100 acres to Thistlethwayte for their specific forest rights, and those present at the meeting where the matter was considered felt that this should be considered as fixed. Thistlethwayte, however objected, and demanded to know why the Crown should have so much more than him. An offer was made to refer the matter to two arbitrators before any application be made to Parliament,[16] and Thistlethwayte agreed, on condition that 'whatever advantages are annexed to the land awarded to the Crown shall be entered to the land awarded to [himself] also'. He demanded that the arbitrators' award be incorporated into the Bill, and that he must be considered to be in the same position as the other purlieu owners as far as other allotments in the enclosure were concerned.

Meanwhile, other parties to the enclosure wrote to Lord Glenbervie, Surveyor General of the Woods, complaining about the delay,[17] and Glenbervie in turn wrote to Charles Taylor, blaming Thistlethwayte and asking for Taylor's help to resolve the matter. He also wrote to Thistlethwayte's agent asking him to obtain the Warden's written consent to the revised terms.

Meanwhile, at a meeting on 15 March 1810,[18] a further dispute emerged. Those present felt that, as land was to be sold for the payment of expenses, though this had not been contemplated when the proposal was originally drawn up, 'the Purlieus of the Bishop of Winchester and Winchester College should bear their just proportion, the Bishop and the College having their allotments ring fenced'. They also objected to a clause inserted by the Bishop of Winchester for the provision of land for the building of a new chapel. As no part of the Forest was more than two miles from a parish Church, this seemed quite unnecessary. The Purlieu owners made it clear that they were 'not happy to prosecute the Bill subject to such a charge', and hoped that the Bishop would be persuaded to withdraw the clause.

The bill was eventually presented to Parliament, and became law in 1810, in spite of a petition,[19] stating that 'any enclosure would materially injure the rights and interest of your petitioners'. Nevertheless, disputes continued. Thistlethwayte, in particular, remained aggrieved, and his representative, Nathaniel Kent,[20] wrote to him on 26 June 1810, apologising that he had not been able to arrange for him to have at least 200 acres. He felt he had done all he could, and blamed the arbitrators, saying that there was 'such a very strong bias in Mr. Driver to the side of the Crown that it was utterly impossible to get the better of it'.[21]

Even when the enclosure was well under way, argument was not at an end. Alex Strong, Thistlethwayte's agent, wrote to him, on 10 March 1812,[22] alleging encroachments by the Crown upon his Purlieu, referring to a perambulation of 1810 as evidence. The dispute apparently concerned approximately one acre of land and 28 trees, and Strong had asked for permission to have the trees cut down and removed into Thistlethwayte's Purlieu. The Crown refused to give way and Thistlethwayte was informed that the fencing would be erected on the original lines. If he wished to pursue the matter he must bring it to court or arbitration.[23] Strong ended with a comment that 'Lord Glenbervie is certainly not behaving handsome towards you in complying with my request'. Thistlethwayte remained recalcitrant,[24] but he had little room for manoeuvre since his major grievance, over the balance between the Crown allotment and his own, had been effectively squashed by the inclusion of the terms in the act. The saga of the Bere enclosure formally ended on 11 October 1813, when the commissioners ordered that the common rights be extinguished.[25]

Other Hampshire examples show that problems and disputes could still occur long after an award had been made, especially if there were any inaccuracies or ambiguities in the commissioners' decisions. A document dated 1857 [26] refers to the Odiham enclosure of 1791, and is signed by:

the persons interested for the time being in the lands inclosed under such local Act and prejudiced by such inaccuracy… in the… award.

The problem arose from the fact that, at the date of the award, Sir Henry Paulet St John Mildmay, the lord of the manor, held land under various different guises. According to the petitioners, he was technically only a tenant for life, rather than the owner, of some of the lands in respect of which he was entitled to receive allotments, 'and he was seised in fee of other lands in respect of which he was so entitled and he was also entitled to some leaseholds'. The commissioners' original award had failed to distinguish properly the different tenures and titles under which the several allotments of Sir Henry should be held, and had set out a single aggregate allotment 'when several and distinct allotments' should have been made. Sixty-six years later this lack of precision was creating difficulties, especially as changes in tenure had taken place in the mean time. Sir Henry had died in 1808, leaving the lands to his widow, who survived him for fifty years. After her death, her trustees felt it necessary to apply for a supplemental or amended award in respect of the fee simple estates, the estates for life and the leaseholds in order to clarify any possible confusion.

The Inclosure Commission was forced to act, and documents dated 1857-59[27] attempted to make a valuation in order to apportion those allotments to the lands in respect of which they were granted. Naturally, the exact positions in the common fields could no longer be pinpointed, although the boundaries of the fields were marked out on a plan, along with the quantities in each field. A second document[28] acknowledged that the award had failed to make any distinction between Sir Henry's settled and unsettled estates. Because the allotments had already been made, 'it was seen that no specific position of allotments accompanied the different titles of these different tenures, so that a title cannot now be made to any part of these allotments'. The commissioners eventually decided that the only equitable solution was to assume that the lands belonging to Sir Henry were of the average value of all the lands in each field, which allowed them to calculate the quantity of land due for each type of tenure. Allotments re-arranged on this basis were set out during 1858.

A similar problem arose with the enclosure of Tadley in 1850. In the preparatory work, a statement from G. Darby to Charles Wellesley dated 1848[29] indicated that:

> a considerable portion of the old enclosed lands in respect of which the right of common exists is copyhold, but the copyhold parcels cannot be distinguished from the freehold, as they cannot be identified by the copy of court roll.

Problems of a similar kind to those experienced at Odiham were forseen, 'since the tenure of the land in respect of which they will be held will be uncertain'. The remedy here lay in the Act 9 and 10 Victoria, cap.70, 6b, which contained a power whereby,

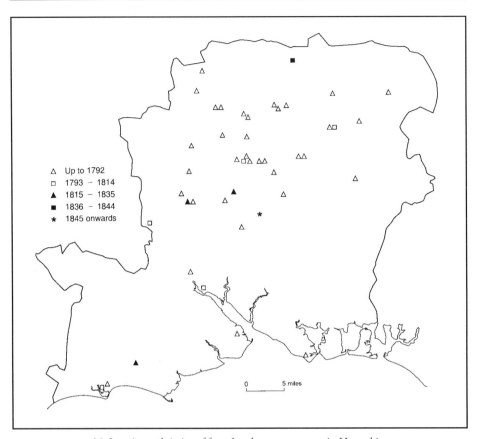

16. Location and timing of formal enclosure agreements in Hampshire.

with the agreement of all parties and the consent of the lord of the manor, the boundaries of copyholds which had been lost or were uncertain could be set out, at a very trifling expense.

Given the difficulties that could present themselves at any stage during the process of enclosure, it is a testament to the abilities of the enclosure commissioners that so many enclosures were accomplished so efficiently. Hampshire, however, seems to have been fortunate in the number of experienced commissioners who were used. No less than 26 commissioners served in this capacity in ten or more parliamentary enclosures, though often with the majority of their work outside the county. This is perhaps a reflection of the number of institutional owners who held land there, since such owners were far more likely to rely on experienced individuals who had worked for them elsewhere, rather than commissioners known and trusted in the local area. Thus Thomas Bainbridge, a favourite Crown nominee, appeared twice in the county, where royal interests were involved. Only five commissioners actually completed ten awards within the county itself, and of these only two, Charles Pink and John Tredgold, followed the traditional model of the local commissioner assiduously picking up every available commission within a very restricted area. The most active individual, George Barnes, fell between the two categories, since he was commissioner to 25 Hampshire enclosures by act, but he was also a favourite nominee of the Dean and Chapter of Winchester, and worked extensively for them outside the county. Perhaps the most significant aspect is that Hampshire had proportionately few individuals who worked on only a single enclosure. Many did three or four, and many had additional experience on formal agreements, so they were able to build up a certain minimal level of expertise.

Formal Agreements

The use of formal agreements in Hampshire has been covered by the authors in an article in *Agricultural History Review*, and full details of the process may be sought there (Chapman and Seeliger, 1995). Since that date a further agreement has come to light, for Oaker Common in Alverstoke, and this has been included in the updated statistics quoted here.

In total, the authors have been able to discover 61 formal agreements, of which 45 date from the eighteenth and nineteenth centuries. As in Dorset, there is some suggestion of an upsurge of activity in the 1690s, with four in this decade, but the peak for this method fell in the eighteenth century, when 36 were concluded. The surge in the late eighteenth and early nineteenth century, when parliamentary enclosure was in full swing, is worthy of note, as is the persistence of agreements into the later half of the nineteenth century (see fig. 17).

It can be seen from the map (fig. 16) that formal agreements tended to be spread widely through the chalklands, but with only a handful elsewhere. The few apparent clusters outside the chalklands are not necessarily significant. Though there were two very early agreements on Portsea Island, for example, there is nothing at all to suggest that they were connected, for they were separated by almost a hundred years, and the one for Fratton was an oddity, carefully disguised as a mere agreement about manorial boundaries (Chapman, 1978). The Island as a whole was certainly undergoing enclosure in the face of urban pressures, but most was informal.

The total acreage enclosed by formal agreement in the county may be estimated at 31,565 acres, of which a projected 23,541 acres, or 2.24 per cent of the total county area, was dealt with after 1700. The sharp fall in the average acreages dealt with is emphasised by the projections for each century. 20,837 acres are projected for the eighteenth, as against only 2704 in the nineteenth.

Hampshire agreements show a markedly different profile from either of the other methods in that they were dominated by open field (see fig. 18). The overall Enclosure Index is 12, as against 47 for acts and 41 for informal means, but 19 per cent of all field systems were abolished by this method as against less than eight per cent of commons. In actual acreages, of those where figures can be calculated, 48.69 per cent was field land and only 47.41 per cent common and waste. Only for the limited number of

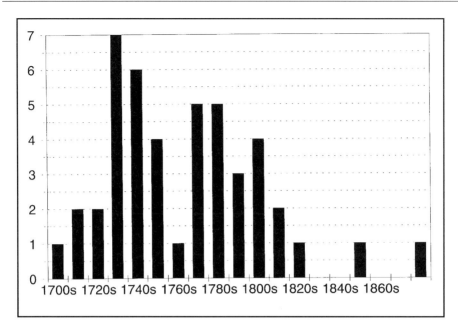

17. Timing of Hampshire enclosure agreements by decade.

nineteenth century agreements does the balance resemble closely those of the other two methods, 30.29 per cent against 63.37, respectively.

In some other respects, Hampshire agreements were not noticeably different from many contemporary parliamentary enclosures. For example, the large and important enclosure by agreement which took place at Goodworth Clatford, on the chalklands near Andover, in 1776-77, shows many of the characteristics of those by act. It involved nearly 1,600 acres of a parish total of approximately 2,800 acres, and was a mixture of common arable, down and pasture, covering three fields and three downs. It followed a common parliamentary format in that it was carried out by three commissioners, Benjamin White, John Brown and Thomas Gale, with a surveyor, Thomas Blandy. There were 18 allottees, of whom four received large allotments, with John Poore getting 404 acres, William Morrant 233 acres, an allotment for pasturage of 226 acres and Peter Head 186 acres. This may be compared with the enclosure of neighbouring Upper Clatford (a parish of 2,209 acres) which took place in 1785, but in this instance following the parliamentary route, and encompassing 1,047 acres of common arable and 30 acres of common meadow out of a total of 1,292 acres. There were 16 allottees, of whom Henry Errington received 504 acres and Charles Rawlinson 302. There is little observable difference between the two.

Other Hampshire agreements mimicked the parliamentary pattern even more closely. The agreement for the enclosure of Nea Common in Christchurch in 1811[30] made provision for public roads, a feature typical of parliamentary awards. Some agreements also make explicit mention of the parallel parliamentary procedures, as at

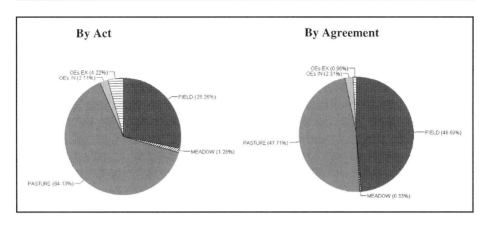

18. Comparison of types of land affected by enclosure acts and agreements in Hampshire.

Milton in 1815, where the parties to the enclosure of Bashley Common[31] deemed that the agreement should be subject to the regulations and provisions of the act[32] as far as the same could apply to the purposes of the agreement'.

The two Clatfords illustrate well the process of multiple enclosures to which a significant number of parishes were subject. A map, made between the years 1743 and 1757, of the manors of Wherwell and Lower Clatford, shows the thin strip fields of the common arable, some having been laid together, next to areas where consolidation had led to the enclosure of long, thin fields with regular, geometric boundaries.[33] Then, following the enclosures mentioned above, they were both affected by a much later enclosure, made under an Order of 1854, of 82 acres of commons.

Other formal agreement enclosures, including some of the earlier ones, appear to show similar evidence of informal activity. An example is the Amport enclosure, whose precise date is actually unknown, but which occurred about 1693, since a surveyor's bill for measuring the three common fields of the manor exists for that date, the last known record of fields there. In addition to the common arable, the Cowdown and a small acreage of the Sheepdown were also surveyed, and Routh (1986) argues that the '88 acres of Sheepdown measured in 1693 is such a small acreage that it may represent the last remnant of unenclosed down'. It seems highly likely that the fields were also merely remnants. The total enclosed was just under 376 acres, of which 260 acres were open field and the rest pasture, out of a parish total of almost 4,000 acres. North Field and Church Field were both just under 100 acres in extent, and the area enclosed in South Field was about 60 acres, all of which were rather small for fully functioning fields in this area. Amport, indeed, has all the hall-marks of a parish already much consolidated and enclosed by informal methods. Only ten allottees are recorded, of whom four received substantial proportions, with Squire Powlett getting 105 acres, Dr. Edes 100 acres, John Drake Goodman 59 acres and William Sweetapple 42 acres. The picture fits well with that outlined earlier, of an area rapidly developing capital intensive farming systems and using formal means to speed up the final phase of enclosure.

Obtaining an agreement was not always a simple process, and Hampshire provides a good example of the pressure which was sometimes exerted to bring reluctant parties into line. In 1787 William Yalden wrote to an unnamed recipient concerning a potential agreement in the parish of Itchen Stoke.[34] The letter is couched in the following terms:

> I take this opportunity… of writing to acquaint you that Mr. Earle and myself with the approbation of the Duke of Bolton and the Duke of Chandos and also of Mr. Smith the Vicar [making together four fifths of the property] have agreed to apply to Parliament the next sessions for a Bill to enable us to inclose Stoke Common Fields. Your brother Farmer Thorn does not seem to approve of it – if he and you consented to the enclosure we should be able to complete our wishes without the expense of a Bill, which would be about a year's rent to each individual – if you do not consent we must then proceed as I have stated to you and whether you consent or not you must pay your share in the expense.

Four-fifths in favour would have been sufficient to secure the passage of a Bill in normal circumstances. The coercive letter must have achieved its aim, because Itchen Stoke Common Fields were enclosed by agreement in 1788

Even when an agreement appeared to have been accepted, its less secure legal basis might encourage some of the parties to prevent its satisfactory operation. This occurred in the early seventeenth century at Wootton St. Lawrence, where the Dean and Chapter of Winchester were lords of the manor. It seems that the enclosures here took effect without any problems for a number of years, but that disputes between the parties, primarily about the feed of the lanes,[35] eventually boiled over into the destruction of gates, hedges and fences. It may seem ridiculous now that major arguments should arise over the use of the grass verges, but at a time when feed stuffs for the over-wintering of animals posed a serious problem, the herbage of the lanes was a matter worth disputing. A series of interrogatories, begun *circa* 1621,[36] reveals that this wrangling rumbled on for a considerable period, since the issue was being re-examined as late as 1631. The Dean and Chapter obviously lost patience with the disputatious tenants of Wootton St. Lawrence, and threatened to reverse the enclosure. In September 1629, they obtained an order of the Court of Manydown manor declaring that all the enclosures in Manydown, Woodgarston, Upper Wotton, Lower Wootton and Ramsdell should be laid open again. The documents make clear that this was done '*in terrorem* to cause the tenants to be quiet', rather than from any real desire to undo the enclosure. There is also a strong suggestion that the dispute was being fuelled by some kind of personality clash, since it is noted that the Dean [had] 'conceived some displeasure against the defendant [William Wither] upon other occasions before he procured this decree'. In the event, the enclosure remained, and the dispute died away.

Though Hampshire made significant use of formal agreements, the question might be posed as to why it did not use them still more. Though agreements could be expensive – almost £668 in the case of Herriard Common, for example[37] – they were normally far less so than acts, and, as has been illustrated, a threat to seek an act was a useful weapon to coerce acquiescence to an agreement. The answer appears to lie, at least in part, in the amount of land held by institutions or by trustees or guardians under family settlements. In such cases agreements were more than usually vulnerable to overthrow, as the North Stoneham case demonstrates, and prudence no doubt dictated that an act should be sought.

Informal Enclosure

The relative importance of informal enclosure in Hampshire after 1700 was considerable. Though it made up proportionately less of the total enclosure than in Sussex, the actual acreage in Hampshire was much larger. Well over 40 per cent of all systems went wholly by this means, and it was particularly significant in terms of common meadows and fields. The vast majority of the meadows, over 63 per cent, used this method, as did over 41 per cent of the fields. Furthermore, as has been mentioned already, many systems were subjected to a substantial degree of informal enclosure before some formal method brought the process to an end. At least 27 open field systems were still partially open at the time of the tithe surveys, including some land in parishes which had already undergone a formal enclosure.

Examples of all the various types of informal enclosure can be quoted from Hampshire, though cases of unification by tenants renting from all the landowners seem to be relatively few compared, for example, with Sussex. Several of the large estates mentioned earlier were able to achieve enclosure by unity of possession, though it sometimes took a substantial period of time. At Bighton, the Duke of Buckingham and his successors were able to completely re-organise and enclose the land in the parish during the years after 1733,[38] and at Ashley the lords of the manor gradually consolidated and enclosed the open fields over a period of two hundred years (see Gilbert, 1992). The landowner might use new leases with a different distribution of plots as a way of re-organising, or changes might be left until some or all of the tenancies fell in hand. Then the land could be reassembled into compact blocks, though this was dependent on the structure of landed estates. In Hampshire, estates are generally rather more scattered than, for instance, in West Sussex, so only small scale re-organisation might be possible. Where most, or the whole, of a parish was held by one family, the landowner could do exactly as he or she wished with the land, even going as far as moving whole villages, though there seem to have been no instances of this in Hampshire during the centuries under consideration. This power enabled many of the major landowners to implement agricultural innovations, and their examples were copied by neighbouring estate owners, encouraging a slow diffusion of new techniques.

Unity of possession was not always easy to obtain, since substantial Hampshire estates seem often to have been intermingled. In these circumstances, reorganising tenancies and waiting for copyholds to fall in would only take a landowner so far, and some form of deal with the neighbouring estate would be necessary to complete the process. This appears to have been the case at Upper Wield, where Sir George Bridges Rodney was unable to complete his consolidation due to the presence of land owned by Lord Portsmouth. Unfortunately, precisely how this was resolved is unclear. A map of Rodney's estates made in 1779[39] provides a tantalising hint at some kind of more formal enclosure. It shows the open fields called White Lain Field, Coppice Field and Middle Field, and part of White Lain Field is marked as an allotment to Lord Portsmouth in respect of estate held by lease of Lord Rodney', while Little Barton and Great Mead are exchanged to Lord Portsmouth. Such wording, and allotments and exchanges, are diagnostic of formal enclosures, yet there appears to be no record of an agreement. However, the fields had apparently gone by 1821, when a surrender to the court refers to lands 'formerly in diverse common fields but now enclosed'.[40] We may be looking at a lost formal agreement, which completed an earlier informal process. Certainly, Bingley's *History* (dated 1807, although parts were written at least a decade earlier), places the enclosure at about the relevant time.

In some cases in Hampshire, it even proved possible to get round the stumbling block of the glebe. The lord of the manor at Abbotts Worthy, the Duke of Bedford, was able to persuade both the rector and the Bishop of Winchester to enter into an indenture to exchange the glebe for three parcels of the Duke's enclosed land elsewhere in the parish.[41] This cleared the way for other parties to remove their land, and almost certainly conduct bi-lateral exchanges themselves. There is a reference in 1798 to Lord Kingston having removed some of his land from the fields,[42] and the fields slowly vanished.

A more direct example was that of Kings Worthy, where the lord, Sir Chaloner Ogle, was involved in negotiations with the same rector, the Rev. Richard Walker, and the Duke of Bedford, who was patron of the living. A formal investigation was held, with six commissioners to investigate the situation, and Ogle presented a petition that the agreement be allowed to go ahead. In it it is clearly stated that

> it is the intention of Sir Chaloner Ogle and the several other parties interested therein to inclose the said common fields,

and it is also noted that the enclosed land being offered in exchange for the glebe was nearly double the value.[43] Again, there is no evidence of any formal arrangements between the others, and the fields merely disappear from the records.

As for cases of owners simply withdrawing their land piecemeal from fields, an extreme example is provided by Portsmouth. This has been dealt with in some detail elsewhere (Chapman, 1978), but the overt nature of the process can be illustrated from an advertisement in the *Hampshire Telegraph* for 1812. This offered for sale by auction a large plot of building land in small lots in the common field of Portsea, 'opposite the land of Mr Radcliffe where a street is intended to be formed'.[44] No formal enclosure had taken place, nor was any intended. The owner was simply assuming that there would be no problem, and that a buyer would be sufficiently confident not to be concerned about any possible legal complications. The effects can be seen on the tithe map of Portsea, where the tattered remnants of the fields are still in being.

The difficulties which might follow from such informal consolidation (and which therefore encouraged more formal proceedings) can be illustrated from Somerford. In 1803 a Mr Covert purchased part of an estate belonging to a Mr Debarry, which included the hamlet of Hubborne. He then bought out the other landowners, and, as sole proprietor, enclosed Hubborne Common. When, however, he in turn wished to sell part of his land some five years later, the would-be purchaser expressed doubts about the validity of his title to the twenty acres of former common included in the sale. In consequence, Covert found himself involved in legal searches stretching back to 1736 to prove that the land had been part of Somerford manor, that the former right owners had been copyhold tenants of the manor, and that the copyholds had fallen in. Elderly witnesses were then needed to testify that no-one else, other than the former owners or tenants of Covert's land, had ever exercised any rights.[45]

A further, and more disputatious, example affected the fields of the parish of Bishops Sutton. There is evidence of a long-continued, and opposed, attempt at informal enclosure here, stretching over at least 50 years. A disagreement arose in 1742 over enclosures 'lately made' in the common fields there,[46] and a memorandum records the nature of the boundaries created. They were evidently quite substantial, since they were built by a mason from Old Alresford, and consisted also of a double fence and quickset hedge, set up by four people. Litigation was threatened in order to secure a 'speedy stop'. Whether the opposition was successful on this occasion is not clear, though parts, at least, of the fields were presumably still open in 1794, when they were included in the act for the neighbouring parish of Crawley.[47] Ultimately they simply vanished, with no evidence of any formal intervention.

In general, informal enclosure was highly favoured in Hampshire. It was simple and cheap to achieve, and, where large landowners were involved, land could often be withdrawn in substantial blocks, even if unity of possession could not be achieved. The existence of a major landowner who was favourable towards enclosure (and if he were not, it could hardly take place) was probably also some guarantee to others who removed their land that the situation would not subsequently be reversed. In urban areas the small plots were often ideal for building, and it was hardly likely that urban houses would be torn down to allow a right owner to graze his stock, however vehemently he might complain. There may have been no one single reason why informal methods were adopted, but they certainly played a major role in the enclosure history of the county.

Summary

Although just over 13 per cent of the county area was subject to parliamentary enclosure, it seems likely that the true total of all enclosure carried out after 1700 was closer to thirty per cent. There can be little doubt that the other methods more than doubled the parliamentary total, and in round figures somewhere between 290,000 and 300,000 acres must have been affected. It is thus far closer to Dorset, and indeed to Wiltshire, than the parliamentary data would suggest.

It is also clear that although overall enclosure was predominantly concerned with common and waste, the agreements and informal methods tended to redress the balance somewhat in favour of open field. It was far more easy to deal with by these means than was waste, and the popularity of informal methods, especially, allowed many fields to disappear without an act.

The fact that so much enclosure was informal does not, however, necessarily mean that a landscape of small farms and fields was produced. In places it was, but informal methods were popular with substantial Hampshire landowners, who were often able to enclose large consolidated blocks in this way. On these they were able to impose a highly regular landscape of large farms and rectilinear fields which differed little, if at all, from the landscapes of parliamentary enclosures. Here, the landscape may mislead, rather than acting as a clue to past development.

6

Sussex

As Dorset forms the south-west apex of the traditional open field triangle, so Sussex forms the south-east; as open fields tended to become rarer to the west in Dorset, petering out towards the Devon border, so there was a similar decline eastwards in Sussex towards the border with Kent. There, however, the similarities end, for physical conditions ensured that few open field systems ever existed in the northern half of the county (Brandon, 1963, p.216) and those which did disappeared early. The Wealden district was basically unsuited to medieval arable farming on any scale, and agriculturally based villages were few: much of the area was used for pasture by the surrounding settlements, and many manors stretched north into the region, or even had outliers within it, to enable them to exploit this resource. Certainly by 1700 open fields were largely restricted to the chalklands and coastal plain of the south, and the north-south contrast was more clearly marked than any east-west one.

The status of Sussex open fields has sometimes been called into question. Though there has been some dispute, the general view is that Kent did not have common fields in the normally accepted sense of the word, and that the Kentish system spread over into parts of Sussex (Baker, 1963; Nightingale, 1952; Baker and Butlin, 1973). Certainly Sussex had its own individualistic terminology, most notably the use of 'laine' for units within the fields, and these laines often appear to have been far more significant as cultivation units than any 'field' in which they nominally lay. Indeed, laine names alone appear in many documents. However, it is clear that field systems subject to communal cropping controls and common grazing rights did exist in Sussex in the period under consideration, that they were more numerous than is often assumed, and that they persisted in remarkably complete form well into the nineteenth century. The West Thorney enclosure award of 1818, for example, makes passing but specific reference to the existence of rights of common over the arable fields, and the Chidham enclosure award of 1812 records that there was a right of common on the fields 'when not sown with Common Grain'.[1] As Map 19 indicates, though there was a slight tendency for the easterly systems to disappear earlier than the western, this was not a universal rule and some of those in the east survived latest of all. Eastbourne, for example, still had remnant fields in 1842,[2] and Piddinghoe had very extensive open areas the following year.[3]

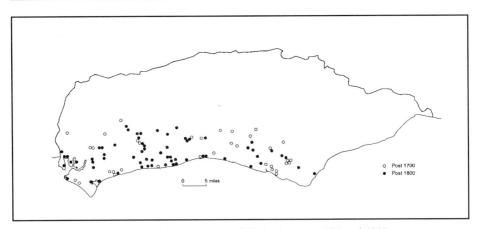

19. Localities with surviving open fields in Sussex in 1700 and 1800.

Exactly 100[4] open field systems appear to have existed in 1700, 70 in the old county of West Sussex and a further 30 in the East. In other words, approximately one third of Sussex's parishes contained open fields of some description at the beginning of the period under consideration, the proportion rising to about forty per cent in the West. It is quite possible that one or two others may have survived undetected into the eighteenth century, for there is ample evidence of other systems operating in the seventeenth, at Coombes and at Wilmington, for example. For Sussex, in fact, the seventeenth century seems to have been a period of significant enclosure, with at least 33, and possibly as many as 70 separate systems being finally enclosed during the century.[5] The idea that Sussex was a county of few open fields in the modern historical period is therefore somewhat wide of the mark.

What is perhaps even more striking is that 64 of these systems were still in existence in 1800.[6] Again, there is some distinction between East and West, since the former retained only 12 (40 per cent) while in the latter almost 75 per cent of the 1700 systems were still there in 1800. The final abolition of open fields, at least in the West, was thus predominantly a feature of the nineteenth century, something not normally associated with the county, which is often assumed to be one of early enclosure. This misapprehension appears to have arisen largely, once again, from an over-reliance on the evidence of parliamentary enclosures. Less than one-third, 32, of the 1700 systems were enclosed by act, with, again, a noticeable distinction between East and West, which will be discussed in more detail later.

As always, putting precise figures to commonable pasture and waste presents by far the greatest difficulties. Hoskins and Stamp (1963) recorded only 1.5 per cent of the county as common at the time of their survey, so that to all intents and purposes any part of the county which had once been common had ceased to be so by the mid twentieth century. The point at issue is the amount which disappeared during the two centuries covered by this volume. Most parishes in Sussex seem to have had extensive areas of common and waste in the Medieval period (Brandon, 1963) and, as has already been noted, in some in the northern Wealden a huge proportion of their area had been rough grazing, though not necessarily always legally common.

By 1700, common and waste can be detected in 215 parishes, while Hoskins and Stamp record them in only 63.[7] Some errors may have arisen in transferring this latter data onto the historic parish base but, even allowing for this, it is clear that something of the order of 150 parishes lost all their remaining common during this period. To this must be added the very substantial acreage lost in parishes which still retained some. Graffham, for example, lost over 1,150 acres, but is excluded since 87.5 acres are listed in the Hoskins and Stamp survey, and Rogate similarly still had 8.5 acres left, having lost 2,915 acres to parliamentary enclosure alone. Much of this enclosure fell in the nineteenth century. Only 31 parishes lost all their common during the eighteenth century, as against 121 in the subsequent 150 years, though this, of course, ignores the significant partial losses.

Though some of the lost commons were small, it is clear that, overall, the total lost greatly exceeded that of open field. The evidence of the parliamentary enclosures is sufficient to indicate the size of many of the commons, for in twelve the amount of common and waste exceeded the biggest open field system enclosed by this means in the county, and many of the others were of the same order of magnitude as the other fields. Such non-parliamentary losses as are precisely quantifiable tell the same story. For example, the lost East (or Tenant) Down at Brighton was recorded at 576 acres in 1790, though 30 acres were in the process of being removed at that time.

Common meadow still existed in substantial quantities in Sussex in 1700, and by no means always in association with surviving open fields. The broad flat river valleys characteristic of the southern and western parts of the county were subject to extensive flooding (as some still are) making them unsuitable for arable use, but well suited to the production of an early lush grass crop, which was greatly prized for the making of hay. For many farmers this was a vital part of their economy, and it is hardly surprising that many parishes clung to their common meadows to a late date. The precise numbers are difficult to calculate, not merely because of the normal problems of lack of records, but also because of some ambiguity of terminology. The term 'common brook' was widely used in Sussex for both a common meadow and wet common pasture land, so it is not always easy in the surviving documentation to be sure to which category any given piece of land belonged.[8] However, the best available estimate is that there were 43 parishes or townships with common meadows in 1700, 8 in East Sussex and 35 in West. 29 of these persisted into the nineteenth century, only two of them, apparently, in the Eastern division of the county.

Some of these meadows were only technically still common in the later period. At Horton (in Upper Beeding) this stage seems to have been reached by 1828, though the meadow did not formally disappear until some time between then and 1842. At Aldingbourne, as in the case of many open fields mentioned in earlier chapters, a single occupier had obtained possession by the time of the tithe apportionment of 1847, though the ownership was still fragmented and common rights were theoretically still in place.[9] However, there is ample evidence that a significant number of these meadows continued to retain fully operational common rights into the nineteenth century, and in some cases even to continue the annual redistribution of the individual plots from which the owners took their hay crop. At Coates this persisted until at least 1830, and may have occurred even later since the meadow was not yet enclosed in 1841.[10] There is no evidence of annual redistribution at Hunston, but rights of common pasture after the removal of the hay crop are specifically mentioned as late as 1871.[11]

The Background to Enclosure

Sussex has traditionally been regarded as a land of large estates, and major landowners such as the Dukes of Norfolk (at Arundel), the Dukes of Richmond and Gordon (at Goodwood), and the Earls of Egremont (at Petworth) were often in a position to enclose without resort to a formal agreement, let alone an Act of Parliament. In many cases, they owned the whole of the open land and were able to reorganise at will when tenancies became vacant. They were also in an ideal position to offer a tempting deal in the form of an alternative tenancy or an exchange of land elsewhere if they wished to proceed in a hurry. This did not, however, mean that such estates necessarily enclosed early. Whether such failures to eliminate the remaining fields were due to a paternalistic attitude towards small tenant farmers, or whether the remaining systems formed too small a proportion of the estate lands to be worth the trouble and expense is not clear. Both may have played a part. In other cases, there is evidence of landowners being frustrated by local circumstances in spite of active preparations for enclosure. As will be discussed later, the Strettington and Westerton open field systems survived into the nineteenth century on the Goodwood estate, though the Dukes had been consolidating holdings for some time. Why they chose not to go for an act to remove the stumbling blocks cannot now be determined, though the ownership of part of Strettington fields by Rumboldswhyke manor may have complicated matters. What is clear is that the great estates were not necessarily in the vanguard within the county as far as eighteenth and nineteenth century enclosure was concerned.

What seems to have speeded enclosure in coastal areas was the rising demand for building land. Many of the remaining open field systems lay immediately adjacent to settlements such as Brighton, Eastbourne, and Worthing which now found themselves rapidly developing as fashionable centres and holiday resorts. The open field strips offered building plots which were gradually taken up, sometimes over a century or more. As will be discussed later, these enclosures were rarely formalised by either agreement or act. Presumably most of the landowners, even if not actively involved in building at a particular time, had an incentive for not opposing their neighbours, since they might well wish to do the same in future. Certainly there is little evidence of opposition, and once building had taken place the prospect of reversing the process and reinstating common rights was a rather remote one, whatever the technical legal position might have been. It may be noted that these systems were often relatively intact and of considerable extent in the early part of the eighteenth century. There is nothing to suggest that most were either moribund or already highly fragmented when the process began. The system at Kingston on Sea may well have been, but those at Brighton and Eastbourne certainly were not.

The coastal systems also faced a physical threat, for much of the adjacent coast was subject to rapid erosion. It is difficult to establish precisely how much was lost in this way, but there are records of the disruption caused by erosion forcing a reorganisation of the system. At West Tarring, for example, Seafield was so badly affected by 1608 that it had been withdrawn from arable use and turned over to use as pasture for the remainder of its existence. Unfortunately, it is not clear how this loss was absorbed by the system; obviously the loss of a whole field must have disrupted any pattern of communal rotations, and Brandon (1963, p. 294) records no references to the other fields in the mid seventeenth century court books, but remnants appear to have been enclosed with Salvington as late as 1811. Bracklesham suffered even more severely, for Brandon records that the fields had been reduced to remnants by 1635, and these apparently vanished shortly after.

With regard to the commons and wastes, there was often little need for any formal procedures, at least in the north of the county. There, the large areas of poor-quality 'waste' meant that there was unlikely to be any very great pressure, and landowners, if they took any notice at all, merely insisted on their rights to a rent from the encroacher. There is also evidence that it was not necessarily the lords who initiated action against encroachers on the smaller commons elsewhere. The case of Horsham has been discussed at length in the literature (Chapman, 1982; Albery, 1927 and 1947), but it is worth noting that the stewards there took no action whatsoever, apparently over a period of 45 years, and it was only as a result of sustained pressure from various local commoners that Charles Medwin, who had become steward in 1787, was pushed reluctantly into holding a manorial court to deal with the offenders. The Duke of Norfolk, the lord, quite specifically distanced himself from the proceedings, leaving Medwin to take any unpopularity which might result. The subsequent manoeuvrings, ultimately culminating in an Act of Parliament, had far more to do with the attempts of various local notables to control the local electorate to further their political ambitions than with any concern with the agricultural effects of encroachments on the common.[12]

The demand for building land was undoubtedly a factor in the enclosure of some of the commons, particularly in the case of some of those in the interior which were of low value for agricultural purposes, but which became potentially highly valuable as towns spread in the later nineteenth century. Ham (1987, p. 221) records that the decision to obtain an act at Storrington was precipitated by complaints of overgrazing, but that Byne Common was rapidly built up once the enclosure had been completed.

Other reasons for the loss of commons occur. Erosion by the sea accounted for some, as at Worthing, where Worthing Common consisted of over 51 acres in 1748 but by the time of the Yeakell and Gardner map of 1780 it had almost gone (Smail, 1949, pp. 56-59). Other examples of this include Cockbush Common, West Wittering, and Middleton Common. There are also occasional oddities. Mee (1913, p. 147) records that Norton Common in Westbourne consisted of 22.75 acres in 1640, but that a substantial part was taken for a mill pond, leaving only 9.38 acres by 1786. Subsequently a further mill pond took most of the rest, and the tiny part that remained was enclosed.

Sussex thus differs somewhat from the other three counties under consideration, both in the intensity and complexity of background influences. While the pressure for building land was a factor elsewhere and was occasionally the dominant force behind an enclosure, in Portsmouth for example, it was much more heavily and widely felt in Sussex. Coastal erosion, at least to the extent of totally removing a unit of common and disrupting a whole system, was a minor but noticeable contributor in Sussex which was lacking elsewhere. It is also arguable that the estate influence was at least as great as elsewhere, and probably more so than in most of Hampshire and Wiltshire.

Parliamentary Enclosure

The details of the parliamentary enclosures of West Sussex were discussed in a paper in 1980 (Chapman), but subsequent events, notably the appearance of a copy of the lost Felpham award,[13] allow some updating of the figures given there. No similar details have appeared in print for East Sussex, though outline details of the acts and awards were compiled by W.E. Tate (1950) and published in revised form in Turner's *Domesday* (Turner, 1978). As part of the research upon which this book is based, details were extracted for every allotment for all parliamentary awards for both divisions of the county, and it is from these that the figures which follow were compiled. The exception is Tangmere, where only a draft award, apparently with some omissions, could be found. This may involve a marginal understatement of the acreage, though the amount is hardly likely to be enough to make any significant difference.

Turner records 88 parliamentary enclosures for the combined county, but only 87 are regarded here as true enclosures. The discrepancy arises from the Barnham award of 1862, under the General Act of 1845, which Turner includes, though noting that the Ministry of Agriculture has no record of it. In fact, inspection of the award[14] indicates that this was purely a reorganisation of land which was already enclosed, with no element of open or common land involved, and it has therefore been omitted from this survey. As Turner notes, doubts might also be expressed about the true status of three of the other enclosures, those for Rye, Ashdown Forest, and Bexhill Down. The first is primarily for the improvement of

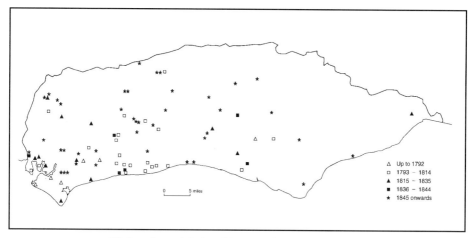

20. Location and timing of Sussex parliamentary enclosures.

Rye Harbour and the other two are essentially regulations of the commons, but since all three seem to have involved some abolition of common rights and conversion of land to individual ownership they have been included here.

From the survey, the total amount of land enclosed within the county was 40,784.00 acres, or 4.37 per cent of the total area. This compares with the figure of 40,969, or 4.38 per cent quoted by Turner, which undoubtedly involves a slight overestimate, and the much older estimate of 3.6 per cent by Gonner (1966 edn, p. 277) which is a significant underestimate. None of the acts for the county was confirmatory, either in whole or in part, though the award totals do, of course, include some already-enclosed land which was exchanged or thrown into the melting pot by the original owners. This total, however, was small, 2,220.56 acres all told, or 5.44 per cent of the land enclosed, though it must be noted that the Houghton award gives no acreages for exchanges between John Brown and the Duke of Norfolk, and details of some Felpham exchanges are also still missing. Once again the two divisions of the county stand in contrast. The smaller western part had 27,800.30 acres, 6.92 per cent, enclosed by this means, while the east had a mere 12,983.20, or 2.45 per cent. Furthermore, almost all the Eastern parliamentary enclosures lay close to the West Sussex border, the main exception being the Rye Harbour enclosure, which has already been identified an oddity in other respects (see map 20).

The type of land enclosed can be determined with some precision. While in some counties awards are confusing or have major omissions, all allotments in Sussex can be assigned to a particular land type, either directly from the text or by the use of accompanying maps. Overall, open field amounted to 8,694 acres, or 21.31 per cent of the total involved, significantly higher than the 6,000 acres estimated by Brandon (1963, p. 318); of this, 7,321.95 acres lay in West Sussex, making up 26.03 per cent of its total, and 1371.88 in the East, 10.57 per cent of all its enclosure. A look at the

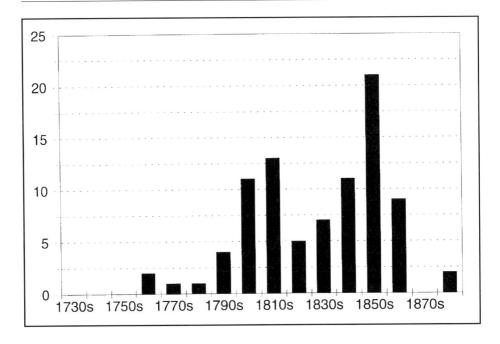

Figs. 21 & 22. Timing of Sussex enclosure acts and orders by decade (above) and acreage enclosed in Sussex by act or order in each twenty year period.

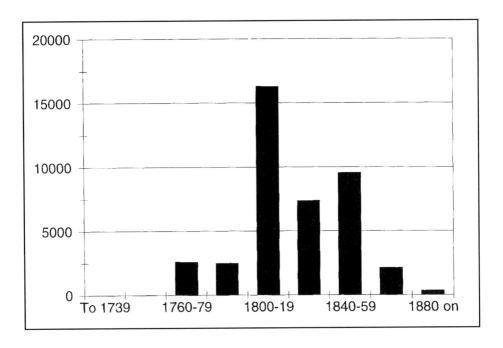

individual enclosures tells the same story. In the county as a whole almost one third of the acts covered some open field, but less than one sixth of those in the East did so, as against well over a third in the West.

The numbers of systems abolished was slightly greater than the number of acts, 32 in all. The Kingston by Lewes act also covered Iford, the Westbourne award of 1823 included the fields of Nutbourne and Prinsted (but not, oddly, of Westbourne itself), and Salvington was dealt with under West Tarring. The remnants of the Worthing system were similarly included in the award for the adjoining manor of Broadwater.

Broadly speaking, the temporal pattern for Sussex fits that outlined by Chapman (1987) for the country as a whole, namely a diffusion outwards from a core in Leicestershire-Northamptonshire. The county was noticeably late in adopting the idea compared with the English Midlands, and there was a general tendency for it to be taken up later the further east one goes. There were, of course, stray late ones in the west, as at Hunston in 1871[15], but East Sussex had only one early one, that at Broyle Park, Ringmer, in 1767, and no more before Telscombe in 1810.

A glance at graph 21 illustrates the overall temporal pattern. From a slow start, acts rose to a peak in the early decades of the nineteenth century, falling in the 1820s and 1830s (though by no means as dramatically as in some other counties), before rising to an all-time peak in the 1840s and 50s, largely as a result of the passing of the General Act of 1845. The subsequent fall-off is precipitous, though enclosure continued even into the 1890s. Comparison with graph 22, which illustrates the amount of land enclosed (by 20 year period),[16] shows a subtly different picture, for although the two peak periods remain the same, their relative importance is sharply reversed. By acreage, the earlier decades dominated, and the 1820s and 30s, traditionally a time of agricultural depression and lack of investment in expensive items such as enclosure, fell not far short of the two subsequent decades.

The logic of this pattern is probably explained by the nature of the enclosure taking place. The Napoleonic period in Sussex saw an upsurge in the enclosure of those parishes which still retained substantial proportions of both field and common waste, and this continued into the 1820s and 30s, including four under the General Act of 1836. The 1845 act, on the other hand, was specifically targeted at land which was either too small in area or too poor in quality to bear the costs of a private act, and in Sussex was used primarily to dispose of small acreages of common.

The contrasts between East and West Sussex can be seen by comparison of graphs 23 and 24 (over), and need little further comment. The relatively later pattern of the East is obvious. However, it is perhaps worth drawing attention to the fact that enclosure acts effectively only arrived in the East at the very end of the Napoleonic Wars, and then continued afterwards, again fitting the concept of a diffusion pattern, but throwing doubts on the effectiveness of the wars as a trigger mechanism.

One very distinctive feature of the parliamentary movement in Sussex is the lack of field enclosures prior to 1800. Whereas in most of the country field enclosure tended to precede that of common and waste, and the eighteenth century was dominated by

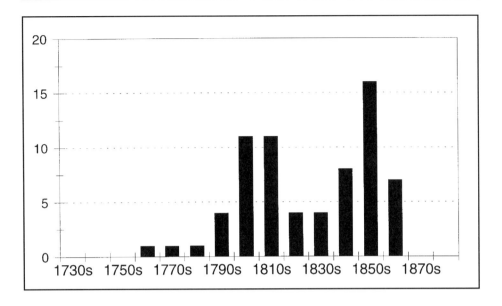

Figs. 23 & 24. Timing of West Sussex enclosure acts and orders by decade (above) and the timing of East Sussex enclosure acts and orders by decade.

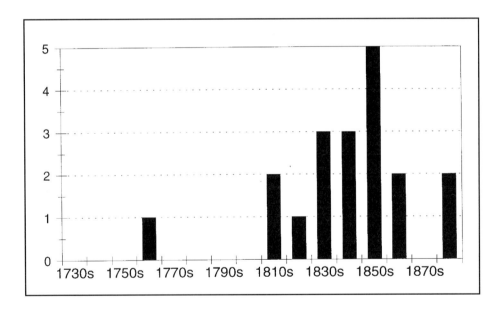

it, in Sussex the first act covering open field, Houghton, fell right at the end of the century, by which time over 12 per cent of the common enclosure had been completed. Precisely why this is so is not entirely clear. As has been suggested, open field formed such a small proportion of most of the large estates in the county that there was ample scope for any experimentation or improvement that they wished to undertake before they needed to tackle systems which could not be easily enclosed without recourse to Parliament.

This is not to suggest that they failed to take advantage of opportunities for consolidation or simplification of the ownership of land and rights when they arose. Apart from the examples of non-parliamentary enclosure discussed later, there are also recorded cases of great landowners buying land and rights, preparatory to, or during the course of, enclosure by act. The Duke of Norfolk, for example, bought out the rights of pasture over Offham Hanger between the passing of the act and the completion of the award. He also purchased the rights which the Bishop of Chichester held on Houghton Down by virtue of his seignory of the manor of Amberley.

The relatively small number of enclosures in the county and the long time period over which they were spread meant that there was a preponderance of fairly inexperienced commissioners. As in all counties, experienced outsiders were occasionally brought in, especially where institutional owners such as the Crown, a bishopric, or an Oxford or Cambridge college were involved, but the vast majority were recruited locally. Thus Sussex enclosures made use of Thomas Bainbridge, a Crown agent and frequent commissioner, Thomas Hopcraft of Crowton, Northamptonshire, and Thomas Fulljames from Gloucestershire, but only Bainbridge served more than once. The most experienced local, Caleb Rickman of Offham, took part in only thirteen enclosures in fifteen years, and in fact completed only twelve, a total which pales into insignificance in comparison with the hundred plus of major figures such as Edward Hare or Richard Richardson. No other local commissioner reached double figures. John Stapley was involved in eight, and James Florance and George Olliver in seven each, which scarcely qualifies them as professional commissioners as the term is understood elsewhere.

This shortage of experienced locals may have had some bearing on the widespread use of non-parliamentary means. Specialist commissioners elsewhere touted for business, suggesting enclosures to local landowners and offering to manage the process for them. Had they existed in Sussex they might well have persuaded more owners to undertake the faster, surer, but more expensive parliamentary road. It is also entirely possible that lack of experience may account for some of the delays in achieving enclosures in Sussex. While Sussex does not show the long delays between act and award found in some Wiltshire enclosures, there is evidence that several proposals hung fire for a considerable period before an act was obtained, even though there was no serious opposition.

Documentary evidence of the period prior to the introduction of a bill to Parliament is inevitably somewhat sparse, but the Amberley enclosure offers an opportunity to gain some insight into the behind-the-scenes activities involved, since the accounts and letters of William Leaves, agent to the enclosure, survive.[17] Leaves notes that he began work trying to achieve an enclosure in 1800, drawing up a draft bill and posting notices. Acting on behalf of a number of proprietors, he spent five years attempting to persuade the lord of the manor (the Bishop of Chichester) and the various proprietors to agree on a scheme, only to abandon it in 1805 in the face of opposition from Lord Selsey, lessee of the bishop's lands, and some other major proprietors.

In 1809, 'Lord Selsey and some others of the former Dissentients now consenting', he made a new attempt. A meeting was finally convened on 7 January 1810 at Houghton, and Leaves then set out again on a long round of visits to the various interested parties to read them the draft bill and obtain their consents. He spent five days at the House of Commons and a further five days at the Lords proving the statements in support of the bill, and on 1 June approached James Florance and Richard Emery, the two commissioners, to sign the notice of the first meeting. He was then obliged to meet them again to formally swear them in as commissioners, and to arrange the appointment of the surveyor (J.S. Hemmingway). It was only then, on 1 October ten years after the first bill had been drawn up, that the commissioner held the first meeting, to arrange for the cultivation of Amberley fields during the enclosure process.

Leaves records 32 formal meetings of the commissioners over the 15 years up to 1825, though, in fact, no commissioner turned up for the meeting on the 16 November 1825, possibly in exasperation at the failure of various proprietors to appear at the two previous meetings to sign their consents to the exchanges which formed part of the award. Several of these meetings took place over a number of days, for example on the 25, 26, and 29 July 1825, and are, of course, in addition to the days worked on the actual division of the land and drawing up of the allotments. Florance calculated that he had spent 79 and a quarter days on the business between 1822 and 1828, charging £2/2½ a day, and Leaves notes that there were 75 days chargeable at £3/3/- against Amberley, 34 against Coldwaltham, and 25 against Rackham, though the period to which this refers is not clear.

There is sometimes an assumption that long-drawn-out enclosures were in fact completed quite quickly, and that it was merely the formalities which held up the final signing of the award, but Amberley illustrates that this was not necessarily the case. Parts of the land were released earlier, for both Coldwaltham Common and Amberley Common were handed over to their new owners in November 1813, but the meetings to give details of the other allotments to the proprietors were not held until 10 and 11 March 1824.

It may be noted that the total expenses for the enclosure are listed as £7,842/15/9½d, of which £5,203/9/7 was borne by Amberley, £1,187/18/3 by Coldwaltham and £1,151/7/11½ by Rackham. This sum was raised by sales of land in Amberley and Rackham amounting to £5,234/16, an initial rate of £1,001/5/11 at Coldwaltham, where there were no sales, and final rates of £738/17/11 at Amberley, £104/18/4 at Coldwaltham, and £344/2/7½ at Rackham. The balance was accounted for by charges to those using the enclosure to confirm exchanges, and by £200 from the Revd John

Hanley. Hanley had agreed to pay this amount as he received an allotment for the small tithes, though a letter from Emery to Leaves points out that Hanley baulked at paying interest on this, and that a further 1d rate would be necessary to cover the shortfall.

From the point of view of the Rackham proprietors, the gain from this process was purely in terms of freedom from tithes. They were allocated no land at all for their former rights on Rackham Common and had to find the sum of £344/2/7½ between them in proportion to the rights which they had had. However, they clearly felt at the outset that this was a worthwhile gain, though unfortunately there is no record of their reaction once the full details became available at the end of the process.

In spite of the initial reluctance of some proprietors, there is little evidence of serious dispute once the process was under way. There were a few disputed claims to common rights, and a certain Mr Hawkins complained about the loss of a road at Coldwaltham, but withdrew his objection after a meeting had been arranged to consider his protest. That, apart from the Revd Hanley's objection to paying interest on what was apparently a voluntary contribution towards the costs,[18] is all that is formally recorded.

Though every enclosure was unique, the Amberley case illustrates a number of common issues. The long build-up, with a good deal of behind-the-scenes manoeuvering and a great deal of hard work by various agents operating on behalf of some of the interested parties was not untypical, as the enclosure of Roughey Manor, Horsham confirms. Similarly, the general lackadaisical attitudes to attendance at meetings is paralleled elsewhere. In most enclosures there were few issues of major significance to the legal claimants, apart from the precise location of their new plots, and most people had better things to do than to travel to meetings to complete formalities. The minor nature of such disputes as did arise is again typical of the majority. Finally, as Amberley shows, matters such as arrangements for eliminating the tithe might be far more important to the participants than mere questions of land *per se*.

Formal Agreements

As with the other counties considered here, the number of formal agreements does not in any way bridge the gap between the numbers of acts and the amount of enclosure actually undertaken. There are the usual problems relating to proposals which may not have been implemented, for example the proposed division of the remaining laines at Falmer in 1800,[19] but even the inclusion of such cases would not greatly alter the picture. All told, there appear to have been only eight in East Sussex and thirteen in West, though a further 12 of earlier date were discovered incidentally during the searches (see fig. 25). Of the 21, twelve were of eighteenth century date, the others continuing as late as 1870, at Rogate Bohunt in Trotton (see fig 26). More surprisingly, only two of the eighteenth century agreements were earlier than 1750, so they clearly did not form a preamble to the parliamentary enclosures of the county. There appears

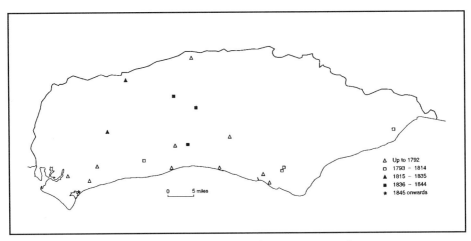

25. Location and timing of formal enclosure agreements in Sussex.

to have been a chronological gap in the use of this method between 1655, when Fishbourne Common was enclosed, and 1717 when there was an agreement for Ifield Common, then a further gap until 1736 when Lancing Down was enclosed.[20]

The use of formal agreements to enclose open fields was even more limited than in the other counties, with only two systems definitely being covered and a further two possibly being involved. Norton in Bishopstone (1766) and Clapham (1812) were certainly enclosed in this way, and there is circumstantial evidence from Seaford and Sutton. In the case of Norton the agreement itself does not appear to have survived, but there is a terrier taken prior to enclosure with notes that the land was then divided and a list of the acreages held by each individual after the division. At Seaford, Brandon records that the whole of the arable was in common fields, and the system was certainly fully operational in the seventeenth century.[21] However, a late eighteenth century map shows the lands enclosed, and notes that it was made 'according to several exchanges which have thereof been lately made', strongly suggesting that it was drawn to delineate the new properties following an enclosure by agreement. If this was so, the enclosure can be dated to 1772, or possibly the previous year.[22]

In Sutton, there is evidence of a scheme to enclose, but it is not entirely clear when, or even if, it was carried out. Open fields certainly existed up to 1827, at which date a plan was drawn up for their enclosure.[23] Leconfield (1954) implies that the scheme was put into effect, but the tithe map and award of 1840 show the land unfenced and refer to plots as 'a piece in... field', a form of words normally reserved for open field;[24] Kain and Oliver (1995, p.527) unequivocally describe it as such. It is hardly likely that owners and tenants would have allowed a document with such financial implications to pass if the holdings shown were not still correct at the time of the survey, so it must be assumed either that the implementation of the agreement was delayed for at least 13 years, or that it was never put into effect in that form. Possibly the contemporary

26. Timing of Sussex agreements by decade.

Lord Leconfield decided to wait in the hope that deaths or land purchases would allow a more advantageous reorganisation.

Clark (1999) has made some play of the very small acreage of open field (19 acres) enclosed by the Clapham award, implying that non-parliamentary field enclosures were generally insignificant, but this was not necessarily so. The Norton award, in contrast, covered just under 276 acres of open field and a further 62 acres of Brook Lands, which would place it firmly into the middle range of Sussex parliamentary enclosures as far as field land is concerned, and above the median in terms of the total amount involved. Seaford covered 302 acres (of open field), and Sutton 188, giving a total of 785 of open field enclosed by this means. If the tiny Clapham award is ignored, the average open field system enclosed by agreement amounted to 255 acres, not very different from the average 292.89 acres enclosed by parliamentary awards.

Having said this, the majority of formal agreements in Sussex were used to enclose commons. Of the 21 agreements only one, that at Norton, did not involve any common, and 12 were concerned solely with it.[25] Again, the acreages involved were relatively modest by the standards of some other counties, but they were by no means negligible. Unfortunately not only do many of the awards contain no areas, but it is not possible in most cases to derive figures from other sources. However, the eight awards which do contain figures give a total of 1818.10 acres, suggesting that something of the order of 4550 acres all told may have been enclosed by formal agreements.

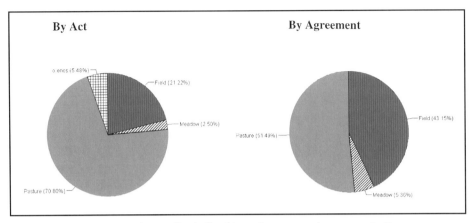

27. Comparison of types of land affected by enclosure acts and agreements in Sussex.

In terms of quantities of land, as opposed to numbers of awards, open arable shows up more prominently, as figure 27 illustrates, but there is need for some caution in interpreting this. Field enclosures are over-represented in those awards containing acreage figures, no doubt because the size of field plots was already known, and it was necessary to show clearly the relationship of these to the reorganised holdings. The four meadows involved may also be an over-representation for the same reason, though the combined total was only 97.5 acres.

For the commons, where acreages are given, the amounts are relatively modest, except in the case of Seaford, where over 526 acres were included. The rest ranged from 42 acres at North Bersted to 104 acres at Westfield. However, these were primarily small commons rather than open downland, and the latter would normally be expected to be larger, as at Seaford. The fact that half the missing 'common and waste' figures relate to downland would thus lead one to suspect that the balance might have been changed significantly had these figures been available. It may well be that the proportions of common to field were not as significantly different from those of the parliamentary enclosures as at first appears.

The agreements where details have survived show a range of different circumstances. At North Bersted the initiative came from the tenants, who petitioned the lord of the manor for a licence to enclose the Brook and North Bersted Meadow in 1789, referees being appointed to oversee the process. At Sutton, on the other hand, the whole scheme was drawn up by the lord, apparently without any reference to an independent outsider, while at Seaford the result was achieved by a series of bilateral exchanges between the landowners. Five awards were certainly made by formally appointed commissioners or referees, and the same is probably also true of Norton. The commissioners were usually three in number and followed the normal pattern of being drawn largely from local yeomen or gentry, and were often assisted by a named surveyor. Three of those concerned, James Bridger of Felpham (North Bersted, Eastergate), Richard Nash of Walberton (Eastergate), and Thomas Hobgen of Sidlesham (Donnington), were also involved in parliamentary enclosures, so it is perhaps hardly surprising that all these awards bear a close resemblance to parliamentary ones.

The situations upon which they had to rule were varied. At North Bersted the shares in the meadow would have been clearly defined, and the lord reserved the right of soil and the manorial rights, so there was no manorial allotment to complicate the judgement. Stocking rights were subject to the *levant and couchant* rule, which was potentially a source of dispute but, in view of the small acreage and the existence of measurable rights in the meadow, the task of creating a demonstrably fair division was not an onerous one. It must be appreciated also that, as so often, these (manorial) tenants were not necessarily small local farmers. Only three were resident in North Bersted, and there was an esquire and two gentlemen amongst them, plus a widow whose precise social status has not been determined.

The Donnington case was a more difficult one, since it was concerned purely with an unstinted common, which therefore had no obvious agreed proportionate interests which the commissioners could use as a basis. There was also the added complication that glebeland existed and had common rights attached, so the vicar's right to commit his successors to the agreement was open to challenge. The fact that the Revd Maurice Smelt died after signing the agreement must have seemed an added complication. However, there was general agreement that the common as it existed 'yielded but small profit to the said parties' so a challenge was unlikely, especially since Katherine Page, the lady of the manor, was also the Improprietor of the parish and therefore able to put strong pressure on Smelt's successors. It was agreed that Page should get one sixteenth for her right of soil, and the problem of compensation for tithes was avoided by the simple device of leaving them in place on the newly enclosed lands.

Eastergate posed more complex problems still. Again, there do not appear to have been clear stinting arrangements, so the decision was taken to use the land tax to determine the proportions of the residue of the common due to each common right owner. However, it was then discovered that some owners paid a single tax assessment for all their lands, some of which had rights attached and some of which did not. It was left to the commissioners to attempt to produce a satisfactory solution.

In summary, formal agreements probably added only a further eleven to twelve per cent to the parliamentary enclosures of Sussex, but they illustrate well the highly diverse nature of the process and the complexities with which the commissioners had to deal. Faced with these, it is hardly surprising that unanimous agreement was often not possible, hence the need for an Act of Parliament in many other cases.

Informal Enclosure

It must be stressed from the outset that 'informal enclosure' covers a variety of different processes in Sussex, and the concept of *an* enclosure date may be inappropriate. Examples of landowners slowly acquiring the whole of the land occur, as do those of the piecemeal withdrawal of strips by individual owners, and there is particularly strong evidence of consolidation at tenant level. In these circumstances, the time-gap between the theoretical legal situation and the practical position on the ground might be substantial. Bits of land might be withdrawn from a field or detached from a common, while rights persisted over what was left, sometimes for a century or more. At Earnley, for example, the fields were apparently long gone as functioning units by 1791, but a single individual still retained a right of common there once the crops had been harvested.[25] Similarly, at Upper Beeding there was technically still one person with common rights on the 300- to 400-acre Common Down in 1886, though these rights seem no longer to have been exercised.[27]

Consolidation at tenant level was often far quicker and easier than the complex pattern of purchases and exchanges necessary to achieve ownership consolidation, but even that might take some time. It was theoretically necessary for a tenant to rent the whole of the common fields or the whole of a particular unit of common grazing in order to suspend the rights. This was certainly achieved on occasions, at Coombes for example, but it is highly likely that in many cases a lower level was all that was needed. Any tenant who acquired the whole of a furlong was almost certainly in a good position to withdraw it from common constraints, and if he gained a whole field the process would have been even easier. Many of the assumptions about the operations of the fields at this period are based on the assumption that because there were often many small owners left, therefore there were a multitude of small farmers, but the Sussex evidence shows clearly that many of these multi-owner parishes were in fact in the hands of two or three substantial tenants. It would have made good commercial sense to such individuals to reach an informal agreement to suspend their rights, withdrawing their stock onto their own grounds, and there seems little doubt that that was what was done in cases such as Heene.

The extent of informal enclosure of the common fields of the county can be readily appreciated from the Enclosure Index. Exactly twice as many systems were enclosed informally after 1700 as were dealt with by act; formal agreements make little difference to this picture. As a starting point, therefore, roughly two thirds of the systems disappeared in this way. Furthermore, there is nothing to suggest that these informal enclosures involved smaller starting acreages than those where Parliament was invoked. Looking at the last scraps remaining when a piecemeal enclosure finally completed its work, or at the few acres involved when owners took advantage of the laws covering the exchange of land in the late nineteenth century can be highly misleading, since by then the systems were in their death-throes. Such details as exist for the early eighteenth century tell a different story, for those systems which were to disappear informally were no different from the rest. Both could be either essentially complete, or already in decay.

However, there is a further aspect which raises still further the importance of the informal processes, for many of the parliamentary enclosures show clear evidence of informal enclosure before being brought to a sudden stop by an act. At Littlehampton, for example, the demesne was already enclosed by 1633 and one field had been laid down to pasture to replace common lost to the sea. Southway Field was 'largely enclosed', but Hampton Hammes and Netherjoy were still open (Brandon, 1963, p.377). The 161 acres which survived to be enclosed in 1841 were thus only the remnants of a much-depleted system, though they included tiny scraps of the same Southway Field which had been 'largely enclosed' over 200 years before. At Prinsted the fields were finally enclosed under an act of 1818, but Breach, Garson and Below Eastope Fields had all been subjected to much piecemeal enclosure over the preceding century. As has already been mentioned, the Clapham enclosure agreement was similarly merely a final tidying up of informal withdrawal of land which was certainly taking place in the late eighteenth or early nineteenth centuries.

The Court Books for Halnaker manor illustrate the process of gradual accumulation by which some common fields disappeared. The systems at Westerton and Strettington both lay within the manor, and there is evidence of a long-drawn-out process of purchase and exchange by which the Dukes of Richmond were able eventually to enclose without formalities. As early as 1743, the then Duke concluded an agreement with the Vicar of Boxgrove, the Overseer of the Poor, and 'divers of the principal Inhabitants of the said parish then present', whereby the Duke surrendered three acres in Westerton common fields for five acres in a field by his park. The agreement included a clause that if the Duke was unable to obtain the rest of the field, the agreement should be void. There are subsequent references to the Duke purchasing land in Westerton fields in 1761 and 1783, and to undated purchases in the 1760s. Similar acquisitions took place in Strettington fields in 1776, 1783, 1785 and 1803, but he was foiled by his inability to gain ownership of the 25.25 acres belonging to the Dean and Chapter of Chichester, and had to content himself for the time being with a 25 year lease of these lands. Legal opinions dated 1809 and 1810 appear to mark the formal demise of these communal systems.[28]

Bramber appears to have had a relatively complete system in 1729, and Bidlington Manor held lands in the West Laine of Bramber in 1690-1. By 1839 these had partly gone, but the western portion still lay in intermixed unfenced strips. However, the tithe documents caught the system at the moment of final extinction, for tenant consolidation had already taken place, and the tithe award refers to the lands as 'formerly called the Laynes'.[29]

Duncton illustrates well the very long time period which might be involved in the process. Brandon (1963, pp. 348-9) records that the ninth Earl of Northumberland had bought up and consolidated much of the land by 1608 and states that only 57 acres of open field then remained. Leconfield (1954), however, states that three common fields existed in 1623. What is clear is that strips were still present in 1777 and that, although one field had been lost nine years later, remnants of other fields survived even then. Similarly, there are records of land being withdrawn from Findon fields from 1542 onwards, but there were remnants as late as 1839 with, significantly, several *occupiers* with intermixed land. There, even at tenant level, consolidation had not been completed after three hundred years.

The typical final stages of a piecemeal enclosure can be seen on the tithe map of Coombes.[30] Here, in 1841, the fields had gone, George Wyndham having gained possession of almost the whole of the parish. Almost, but not quite, for intermixed amongst his land in the former open fields were 16.75 acres of scattered strips belonging to the glebe. Characteristically, the problem had once more been solved at tenant level, for John Hampton, a fifty-year-old farmer from Applesham Farm, occupied the land of both owners.

The Fulking tithe map shows a slightly earlier stage. Just under 21 acres of open field remained, but the adjacent area has all the signs of recent enclosure, with three occupiers and two others apparently working in common.

The final tidying up of the system often involved the exchange of land which had already lost any communal function, and which might even have been physically fenced, but in scattered plots of awkward shape. At Storrington, Brandon (1963, p. 351) mentions piecemeal enclosure in 1615, but open field still survived in South Clays and The Springs in 1811. By 1841 they had been enclosed, but it was not until 1864 that a formal exchange of lands removed the vestiges of scattered ownership which piecemeal enclosure had left behind.[31]

Piecing together the gradual eating away of the commons is almost impossible. Some rentals, such as that of 1766 for Balneth manor, meticulously indicate land which was formerly part of the lord's waste,[32] but there is no question that many encroachments were never recorded as such. The numerous permissions to enclose which appear in the surviving court books and incidental papers of the lords and their stewards must represent only a fraction of those which were granted, but what fraction it is impossible to say. Many of the individual grants were very small, such as the rood of land at Alciston mentioned in a note of 1802 from William Wood, who had measured the plot so that Thomas Gossden could present a request for permission to enclose to the next session of the Alciston court.[33] On the other hand, some far larger plots appear. A rent roll for Barcombe of 1734 mentions two parcels of land 'heretofore inclosed' from Handly Common and totalling 60 acres.[34] Further examples come from Maresfield, where a surrender of 1751 makes a distinction between 'assert lands' and 'new assert lands', and there is a record from 1772 of the tenants consenting to Robert Hoath enclosing 2.75 acres of the waste of the manor.[35] More references occur in the Adams manuscripts, which cover a number of very extensive commons, and which show their gradual diminution, for example at Hailsham and Framfield in 1646. There are also references to 'new inclosures of the commons and wastes' at Allington, and to 130 acres of 'The Common waste called the Beechwood inclosed' and leased for 1000 years.[36]

Much enclosure of the common was carried out without permission, and prosecutions for encroachment are often mentioned. For example, William Washer Esq. and his tenants, John and Thomas Ade, were presented at a General Court Baron of Alciston, dated 13th June, 1783 for enclosing half an acre of land at the bottom of Wincton Street in Alfriston 'being part of the waste and to which the tenants had right of commonage'.[37] The Beadle was ordered to cut down the fence, though it is not clear that this was ever done. Certainly elsewhere the same individuals were prosecuted time and time again for the same offence, but nothing was actually done to reverse the encroachment.

As in the fields, the gradual fading away of rights was undoubtedly a major cause of the loss of commons. It is often assumed that these were formally accumulated by the lord of the manor, and this certainly occurred. For example, the 433-acre Hangleton Sheep Down was apparently all in the hands of one individual by 1790, though common rights had certainly been exercised by several right owners in the past. In other cases, however, it seems that individuals simply failed to use their rights over such a long period of time that they were eventually forgotten, or at the very least became impossible to verify, should any individual have wished to re-establish them. Hoskins and Stamp (1963, p.328) record that Chapel Common, of over 300 acres, was mostly ploughed and fenced, and that the remaining rights were 'doubtful'. The 215 acres of Linchmere Marsh and Common were 'agriculturally unused', and thus fall into the intermediate stage, where rights were still known or believed to exist but were in danger of being lost due to lack of interest in retaining them. Similar situations can be detected in the two centuries under detailed consideration in this volume. For example, it was recorded that in 1886 there was still technically one individual with rights on the Common Down of Upper Beeding, though the wording implies that they were not then being exercised.[38]

Often it is by no means clear how land came to be removed from the commons, merely that it had happened. References to parts of Common Downs, especially, as 'now ploughed up', while the remainder was still in common use, are frequent. At Litlington, the open fields were enclosed by agreement in 1634,[39] but the Sheep Down continued in common for a further two centuries. In 1844 it appeared to be still there, but part is shown as 'broken up', apparently foreshadowing its imminent disappearance.[40] Similarly, 30 acres of Brighton Down are marked as tillage in 1790, though parts persisted long after.[41] Others can be firmly established as existing at one date and gone by another, though whether piecemeal or at a single stroke is unclear. The 148 acres of Bramber Free Down were open in 1729, but by 1839 they had gone, though the Tenantry Down and other areas remained open.[42] It may well be that a similar process had operated to that at South Bersted, where the recent deposition of the Raper Papers reveals that the vanished commons were in fact enclosed by the manorial tenants under a licence from the lord of 1789.[43]

Summary

In one respect the enclosure history of Sussex seems to have closely resembled that of Hampshire, since it, too, shows non-parliamentary enclosures exceeding those by act after 1700. Some nine per cent of the county was subject to enclosure, more than doubling the parliamentary total. However, formal agreements contributed even less than in Hampshire, and it was informal means which made up the bulk of this extra amount, thus differentiating it to some extent from what happened in the adjoining county.

The informality of the methods tended to produce the expected results, namely small fields and continuing fragmentation of landownership, and elements of this survive to the present day. Much of this was, however, relatively short-lived. Urbanisation soon obliterated a great deal of the resulting landscape in the coastal areas where so much of the informal field enclosure had taken place, and the dominance of large estates ensured that a good deal of the rest was consolidated in the later nineteenth century. The small absentee landowners described earlier had little incentive to hang on to their plots as the social and economic situation changed, and there was ample opportunity for larger landowners to round off their estates. Thus it is largely the results of informal enclosure of common wastes which tend to survive today, and even these have undergone substantial change as urbanisation has marched into these areas as well. The descendant of the eighteenth century waste encroachment is today as likely to be a large detached mansion as an agricultural smallholding.

7

Wiltshire

Of the four counties under consideration, Wiltshire is, on the surface, closest to the conventional picture of enclosure in the eighteenth and nineteenth centuries. A very high proportion of the parishes had an enclosure act, and a high proportion of those acts was concerned, at least in part, with open field. Many of the acts covered a substantial proportion of the parish involved. In these respects the county bears a strong resemblance to the Midland counties, such as Leicestershire and Northamptonshire, from which so much of the conventional picture has been derived. The peak of parliamentary activity was somewhat later, clustering in the 1800s and 1810s, but this is hardly surprising if the suggestion of a diffusion pattern is accepted, given Wiltshire's distance from the core (Chapman, 1987). The extended period over which major enclosure activity took place also seems unexceptional, given the county's substantial north-south extent.

Wiltshire, however, differs in a number of respects from the typical Midland open field model. The dominance of chalk uplands in much of the south and east of the county meant that many open field parishes had very substantial areas of common grazing on the open downland, with the arable restricted to the valleys and the neighbouring lower slopes. Furthermore, the chalk downland offered the possibility of at least short-term reclamation, giving a flexibility to the distinction between arable and pasture land which seems to have been largely lacking in the Midlands. Examples of temporary conversion of parts of the down to arable, and of new open fields being created from the down to replace those enclosed and converted to individual ownership are not uncommon. These can be illustrated from Collingbourne Ducis (Kerridge, 1967, p.48) and from Winterbourne Dauntsey respectively.[1] In 1726, the three fields at West Grimstead were reorganised into four, with forty acres of the down being added to make them large enough.[2] In this respect, Wiltshire is closer to East Yorkshire than to Northamptonshire.

Many of the parishes of northern and western Wiltshire also had extensive commons. The historic county stretched into the limestone of the Cotswolds, which were agriculturally not dissimilar to the chalklands, and marshy or heathy commons occurred elsewhere. The basic assumptions behind many accounts of Midland enclosures, namely that there was a shortage of pasture, and that incorporating the commons into the intensively farmed area made little difference to the acreage, do not apply here.

Putting a precise figure to the number of field systems functioning at any given date presents even greater problems in the case of Wiltshire than for the other three counties. Many of its parishes had multiple systems, and it is not always possible to distinguish these clearly in the surviving documents. Small independent systems were sometimes later combined with their neighbours, further confusing the issue,[3] and the absence of complete documentation in some of the surviving agreements makes it difficult to determine whether they covered one or more systems. As was so often the case elsewhere, many systems showed a progressive collapse, rather than passing directly from a fully functioning entity to oblivion as a result of a single act of enclosure. Moreover, Wiltshire seems to have been particularly prone to acts which, in whole or in part, confirmed enclosures already carried out by other means, and to acts covering several systems at once. Whether a series of agreements and acts represented a gradual dismantling of a single system, the enclosure of different tithings or townships within the same parish, or merely successive confirmations of the enclosure of the same land, is often difficult to determine. The four agreements and two acts referring to the parishes of Great and Little Bedwyn, illustrate the problem.[4]

In Wiltshire there are particular problems in pinpointing the moment of enclosure even when an act was used, due to the extraordinary length of time which it took to complete many of them. Long delays occasionally occurred elsewhere, as at Horncastle in Lincolnshire (48 years, see Turner, 1978, p.166) or Caerwys in Wales (41 years, see Chapman, 1992, p. 88), but in Wiltshire there were 21 cases of delays of ten or more years between act and award, seven of them taking more than 20 years. It is thus not always clear precisely when a system finally ceased to operate, since it certainly cannot be assumed that it continued up to the time of the final award. In the case of the common enclosure at Broad Chalke, it is specifically recorded that the allottees had occupied their new allotments long before the final signing took place in 1861, but exactly when this occurred is uncertain (Ellis, 1971, p. 47). The same is true of most of the other examples of long delays: they were probably completed *de facto* some time before the end of the legal formalities, but one cannot be entirely sure.

All this is in addition to the normal problem of long gaps in the records, which often straddle periods of particular interest. For the purpose of this study, those stretching from the late seventeenth into the early eighteenth centuries are particularly frustrating, though in this respect Wiltshire is fortunate in the survival of a good many glebe terriers of 1704, which serve as a useful starting point. However, even when terriers exist, this does not solve all problems. Did Kington St Michael's fields, existing in 1671, or those of Yatton Keynell, recorded in 1698, survive into the eighteenth century? Both were apparently gone by 1704.[5] In fact, it is clear from the records that Wiltshire was undergoing a significant period of field enclosure which straddled the end of the seventeenth and the beginning of the eighteenth centuries. There were formal agreements for Ludgershall in 1682, Tockenham in 1699, and Stitchcombe in 1703, for example.[6] Stating precisely how many systems were operational at the arbitrarily chosen date of 1700 is thus open to some margin of error.

Bearing these problems in mind, it seems that 288 systems were in existence in the county in 1700, of which just over half, 146, still survived in 1800. As map 28 illustrates, they were widely spread throughout the county, especially when it is appreciated that the locations shown are those of the settlements to which the systems were attached, and that many of the apparent gaps merely reflect the distribution of the extensive common downs already referred to. These formed integral parts of the systems of the adjoining valley settlements, but adjoined each other in the higher areas, giving rise to many blanks on the map. This applies also to the Dorset border area, where the commons of Dorset and Wiltshire parishes met on the border ridges. There is, however, a noticeable band running north-east to south-west across the northern part of the county, which does appear to represent a significant patch of settlements where fields were lacking. Smaller gaps occur in the heathy lands of the north-central part of the county, and in the south-west along the border with Somerset. The former may well be due to the unsuitable nature of parts of this land for open arable; in the latter case, the landownership pattern, which will be discussed later, may have been a contributing factor.

The pattern of loss between 1700 and 1800 is of some interest, since although enclosure was significantly greater in the east-north-east, as the national parliamentary diffusion model might suggest, there are clear groupings elsewhere. Open fields disappeared almost entirely from the Ebble Valley in the extreme south of the county, and a similar grouping can be seen in the south-west. These two illustrate some of the factors which complicate the generalised national pattern when one attempts to apply it at a local level. In the former case, for reasons which are not entirely apparent, a local diffusion of the idea of parliamentary enclosure seems to have taken place. The idea was taken up enthusiastically by adjacent parishes, to such an extent that multi-parish enclosures took place, covering several parishes in the same act. One such act involved almost 15,000 acres, and substantial parts of eight parishes. This was unusual, nationally, and was certainly helped by the fact that a number of owners held land in more than one of the parishes concerned, most noticeably the Earl of Pembroke. However, it cannot be solely attributed to the direct influence of a single owner, since none held land in all the parishes, not even the Earl.

The second grouping is more straight-forward, since it lies in the heartland of the Longleat estate, which was undoubtedly the major motivating force. Many of these enclosures were achieved by private agreement, though they frequently mimicked parliamentary awards very closely in their form and procedures. The process was no doubt helped by the presence of Thomas Davis, steward to the Marquis of Bath, and a highly experienced enclosure commissioner, with at least twenty parliamentary awards to his name, in addition to several agreements.[7] Davis was used both to the formal procedures themselves and to the negotiations with the various parties which were an essential preliminary to either an agreement or an act, and his experience would undoubtedly have smoothed the way for enclosures on his employer's estates.

Common pastures are even more difficult to enumerate in any meaningful manner. Intercommoning certainly occurred, and small hamlets lying within a parish

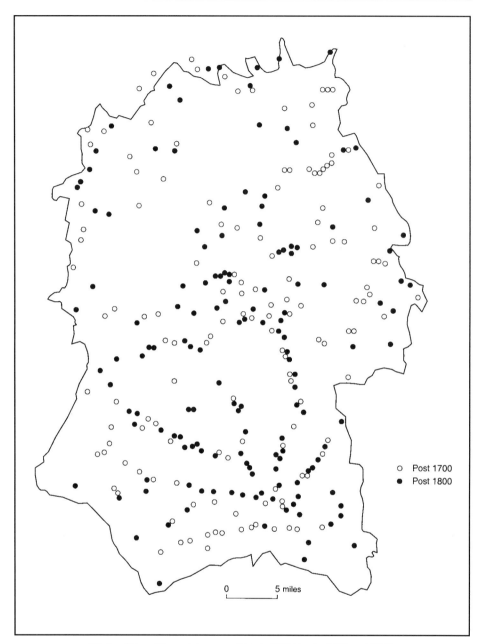

Post 1700 ○
Post 1800 ●

28. Localities with surviving open fields in Wiltshire in 1700 and 1800.

might, or might not, have commons for their exclusive use. It is often unclear from the surviving documents, particularly the enclosure acts and awards, whether the various townships and manors mentioned were separate entities for this purpose, or whether all their freeholders and customary tenants had access to the same single group of commons. However, the best estimate is that 292 townships, manors or parishes had separate groups of commons in 1700. This is effectively almost the same total as for open fields, but the actual units concerned were not necessarily the same. For example, it is not clear whether Broughton Gifford's open fields survived into the eighteenth century, but some of the common persisted into the modern period (VCH, VII, pp. 51-2 and 58; Hoskins and Stamp, 1963, pp. 333-5). 189 of these 'systems' have been detected in the nineteenth century, and 28 remained to be listed by Hoskins and Stamp,[8] though in almost all cases very substantial losses of acreages and of one or more parts of the system took place in the intervening period. Parliamentary enclosures, for example, frequently excluded parts of the common, whereas it was unusual to omit parts of the fields.[9]

Meadow land has long been recognised as playing an especially important part in Wiltshire agriculture. A physical environment well suited to keeping large numbers of stock on downland pastures inevitably created a heavy demand for winter fodder if it was to be exploited to its maximum extent, and the river valleys cutting through the chalklands provided the ideal means of supplying this. The relative warmth of the water seeping out of the chalk in early spring ensured an early start to grass growth, ideal for hay production, and it is no surprise that Wiltshire was one of the pioneering areas in the country of the artificial flooding of water meadows. Kerridge (1967, p.40) has gone so far as to suggest that this was a key element in the 'Agricultural Revolution'. Not all such meadows were common, but, in the circumstances, the presence of large numbers of common meadows in 1700 is hardly unexpected.

Since common meadows, like pastures, could quite easily operate independently of any other communal elements, they might continue long after the fields had gone, as at Chippenham, or be enclosed before them, as at Alderton. There is therefore an element of doubt as to precisely how many existed at the beginning of the eighteenth century, and especially how many parishes or townships possessed them. The best estimate is that there were 144, of which 82 survived a century later. According to Hoskins and Stamp (1963, p. 334), Urchfont still possessed one in the middle of the twentieth, though it is there described as 'wet pasture'.

The meadows varied enormously in size, especially in the later part of the period under review. When land at Corsham was enclosed in 1819, the total of meadow and pasture together was only 36 acres, while the Lammas Mead at Enford is recorded at over 1000 acres. Significant numbers of the meadows are described as 'lot meadows', and there is evidence of continuing redistribution well into the eighteenth century. Coate Lot Mead in Liddington, for example, was still being redistributed by drawing lots in 1766.[10]

The Background to Enclosure

Wiltshire has some claim to be amongst the most idiosyncratic of all counties, in terms of its enclosure history after 1700. There seems to have been a peculiarly Wiltshire reluctance to actually carry an enclosure through to its logical conclusion, such that the distinction between 'enclosed' and 'open' is even less clear-cut than elsewhere. The definition of not only agreements but also acts as 'enclosures' is sometimes dubious, and lands apparently subject to a formal enclosure might often have most of the characteristics of open and common lands long afterwards. The Quidhampton agreement award of 1798, for example, reallocated common fields, common meadows and common pastures, but ended by specifying the arrangements for feeding the fields in common after the harvest, thus effectively reinstating the communal arrangements, but on larger plots.[11] Similarly, the award for Netherhampton under the act of 1783 ordered that the 'newly-enclosed' fields should be separated by 'linches', and should continue in a three-course rotation by field, and that the down allotments should be fed in common.[12] There are certainly examples in other counties of awards leaving some land in common, of land being allotted but left subject to common rights until the owner chose to fence his own plot, and of fencing being voluntary (Chapman, 1976), but the sheer numbers of partial or 'not quite' enclosures seems unique to Wiltshire.

Many of the local peculiarities of Wiltshire enclosures can be traced directly to the traditional forms of agriculture practised there and, at one remove, to the physical environment in which agriculture took place. Mention has already been made of the significance of meadowland, and especially of the early and multiple hay crops obtainable through the technique of flooding water-meadows. From this derives the meticulous arrangements included in, for example, the Sherrington agreement to ensure that the water-meadow system would be able to continue.[13] Many parliamentary awards show a similar concern, for example those for Ebbesborne Wake (1792), Bishopstrow (1811) and Corton in Boyton (1829).[14]

More significantly, enclosure posed a threat to the mainstay of Wiltshire's chalkland agriculture, the sheep flocks. In many villages the open fields lay on the lower chalk slopes, on soils which were thin, which lost fertility rapidly when cropped, and which were apt to dry out excessively in the summer. The ability to maintain these lands in arable cultivation was highly dependent on the dung provided by the flocks which were folded on them, and which, in addition to providing fertilizer, gave bulk to the soil and slowed down the natural rapid percolation of water through them. For small tenants, at least, the division of both down and field into small hedged plots was potentially disastrous. Keeping one or two sheep on a small downland allotment was neither a practical proposition nor a means of supplying sufficient dung to maintain the arable. It was no doubt primarily for this reason that so many Wiltshire enclosures, mainly formal agreements, designated parts of both the down and the fields to continue in communal use by some of the manorial tenants. Such an arrangement would have seemed a curious half measure to contemporary enclosers elsewhere in the country, but was a sensible, if temporary, adaptation of the process to local conditions. It also seems highly likely that Wiltshire's greater reliance on formal arrangements than the other three counties was in part due to this cause. Informal enclosures elsewhere usually produced precisely the type of tiny plot which would have been quite unsuited to this type of agriculture: use of a formal act or agreement allowed a more thorough-going reorganisation.

Having said this, the role of local habit cannot be disregarded. Any study of enclosure over a wide area of the country rapidly reveals local quirks derived purely from the unsurprising tendency of local people to adopt methods with which they were familiar. For the most part, they tended to copy earlier neighbouring examples, and drew on existing local expertise to guide them through the process. Thus, while the origins of the Wiltshire approach may be logically explicable, the early development there of a small group of highly experienced commissioners must have encouraged its use in other parishes. Such men were familiar with the complexities of obtaining an enclosure by act, and had a vested interest in recommending it to potential enclosers, since it was likely to lead directly to further employment opportunities. Richard Richardson, whose role as a commissioner will be discussed later, also worked extensively as a surveyor and valuer of estates, and no doubt took every opportunity to draw the owners' attention to the potential gains from enclosing the lands, as he certainly did in other counties. Another active commissioner, John Tredgold, is specifically recorded as doing so in Wiltshire, for when he surveyed Longstreet Farm, Enford, on behalf of the Dean and Chapter of Winchester in 1798 he appended a note that the estate lay in common fields 'and would greatly improve by enclosing'.[15]

Parliamentary Enclosure

The parliamentary enclosures of Wiltshire have been extensively covered in two works. Firstly, Sandell's list (1971) provides a detailed coverage of each award, including a total acreage and substantial details of the lands enclosed, indications of those to whom the land was allotted, and listings of the commissioners and surveyors who undertook the work. This listing is invaluable as far as it goes, but it unfortunately omits those enclosures for which no award is known, even though acts exist. It also deals with each award separately, in contrast to the normal convention, as adopted by Tate (1944) and Turner (1978), of treating each act or order and its whole outcome as 'an enclosure'. Wiltshire, more than most counties, tends to have several awards from a single act, perhaps because acts frequently covered several parishes or separate field systems. There is thus some confusion between Sandell's and Turner's listings, and for consistency with the other counties, and with the National Enclosure Project database, Sandell's material has been re-assembled into the conventional format where necessary for comparative purposes.

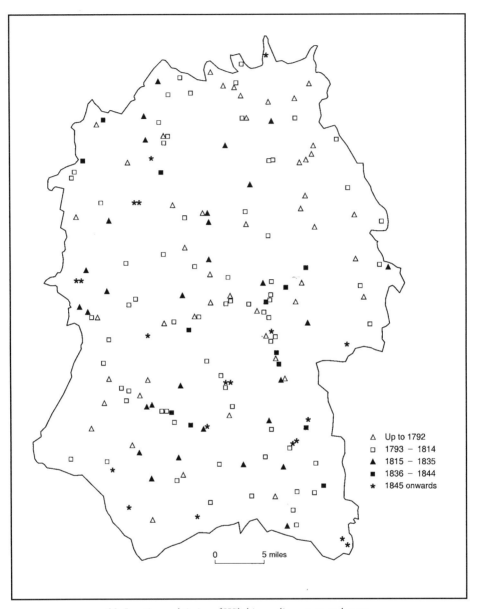

29. Location and timing of Wiltshire parliamentary enclosures.

A second major work is that of Ellis (1971). This is ostensibly concerned with parliamentary enclosure and provides a great deal of data about, and insight into, that aspect of Wiltshire's history. However, it goes rather further than its apparent brief, and contains extensive comment on aspects of non-parliamentary enclosure as well. Ellis has also published material on the widely neglected later phase of the parliamentary movement, namely that part under the General Enclosure Acts of 1836 onwards (Ellis, 1980). Both these offer more detail than can be contained in a volume of this length.

Parliamentary methods dominated the pattern in Wiltshire in a way which they did not do in the other three counties. In terms of the Enclosure Index, almost 73 per cent of all units were finally disposed of in this way, as opposed to just under 16 $\frac{1}{2}$ per cent by informal means and $10\frac{1}{2}$ per cent by formal agreement. As the earlier discussion makes clear, the peculiarities of Wiltshire enclosure grossly understate the informal element, but, even allowing for this, the contrast with the other three is most marked.

Altogether, there were 181 individual parliamentary enclosures (as defined above) in Wiltshire. This accords with Turner's figures, but there are two discrepancies. Firstly, Turner excludes the award of 1856 for Tytherton Lucas in Chippenham, noting that he was unable to find any other reference to it, though it was supposedly under an annual General Act (Turner, 1978, p. 278). In fact the reference to a General Act as the authority for the enclosure was probably to those of 1836 and/or 1840, which would not require confirmation by an annual act, and this enclosure has been included here. Secondly, Turner includes in his total the act for Cranborne Chase, noting it, correctly, as being in both Wiltshire and Dorset. However, in order to avoid double counting, the National Enclosure Project database classifies it under Dorset (enclosure number 10033), since the great majority of the land involved lay in that county. The actual acreage given in the award as lying in Wiltshire has, however, been included in the county totals given below.

The parliamentary movement in the county stretched in date from 1725 (the act for Compton Bassett) to 1883 (final award for Upper Seagry and Christian Malford). As was frequently the case in other counties, the earliest date is misleading, for there was something of a false start. The Compton Bassett act was purely to confirm an existing agreement, as was one of only three acts passed in the 1730s, that for Stanton. In effect, parliamentary enclosure did not really take off in the county until the 1770s, after which it was continuous through until the 1860s, by which time the overwhelming bulk of the enclosure which was to take place had already been initiated.

The temporal pattern is in fact one of the closest to the statistician's 'normal curve' of any county (see Fig. 7.3). The very marked peaks and troughs visible elsewhere are effectively reduced to a sharply rising trend up to the 1810s, followed by a steady fall until the completion of the process. Of particular interest, perhaps, is the very large number of acts passed between 1810 and 1819. Conventional explanation of the chronological pattern tends to lay stress on the significance of the Napoleonic Wars, both as a stimulating factor while they were being fought, and as a cause of a sharp fall when they came to an end. However, there is no indication of any such fall in

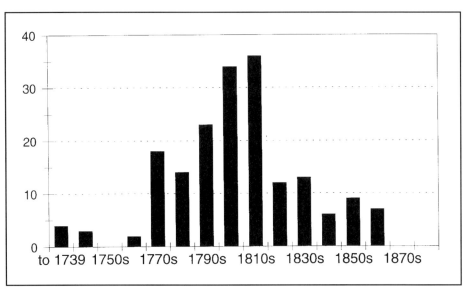

30. Timing of Wiltshire enclosure acts and orders by decade.

Wiltshire. The peak in the 1810s is no mere artifact of a bulge in the last years of the war, or of a hangover of acts still making their way through the procedures after the war came to an end: no less than seven acts were passed in 1818-19, long after the wartime effects had vanished.

Spatially, also, Wiltshire shows a relatively simple pattern. The initial phase of parliamentary enclosure in the county, prior to the Napoleonic Wars, shows widespread patches of activity (see Map 29). As the diffusion theory would suggest, the north-eastern areas were particularly affected, with almost all acts passed prior to the outbreak of war and the rest completed shortly afterwards, with the exception of Rodbourne Cheney, Marston Maisey, and Froxfield. Elsewhere there was, as might be expected, significant progress in the villages on the northern and eastern fringes of Salisbury Plain, and also a cluster in the area round Warminster, no doubt associated with the contemporary agreement enclosures on the Longleat estate.

The War period effectively spread parliamentary enclosure to the whole of the rest of the county, leaving a substantial (but geographically fairly dispersed) number of parishes to be dealt with in the post war period. Though there are some minor clusters, in the valley north of Salisbury for example, it would be straining the evidence to suggest that they had any real geographical significance. Several, indeed, had been the subject of earlier enclosure attempts but had been thwarted for purely local reasons. Marston Maisey, for example, had apparently been the subject of an attempt 51 years earlier, and certainly of another 35 years before enclosure proved possible.[16] The whole picture is one of a fairly rapid and complete adoption of acts as a normal means, once the idea was established.

Unscrambling precisely how much land was affected by parliamentary enclosure presents particular problems in Wiltshire. As has already been mentioned, an unusually high number of acts appear to have been confirmatory, either in whole or in part, of an enclosure which had already been completed. Turner (1978) records five in the former category and two in the latter, and additionally the act for Everley in 1816 appears also to have been purely confirmatory. Doubts exist about others, such as the act for Great and Little Bedwyn mentioned earlier. Conventionally such enclosures have been regarded as parliamentary, but this may introduce an element of double counting, though four of the acts concerned do not in fact contain any acreage. There may also be some distortion of the temporal pattern of enclosure, though only the Everley act, 36 years after the agreement, seems to have been more than a year or two later.

The best estimate that the authors have been able to derive is that 256,458 acres, or 29.68 per cent of the county, was affected by parliamentary action. This total includes that part of the Cranborne Chase enclosure which the award notes as falling within the county of Wiltshire. It may also include some small areas which actually lay outside the county boundary, since Wiltshire had several enclosures which straddled the then-existing border, and it is not always possible to assign these lands to the correct county. The total has been compiled by summing all allotments in the ten per cent sample of awards in the National Enclosure Project, plus figures drawn from the works of Ellis and Sandell mentioned earlier. For three of the four enclosures where there is no award and the act gives no figure, estimates have been made from what can be gleaned about the amount of land lost during the period. For Everley, it has been assumed that the act was confirming the agreement of 37 years earlier, and the figure from the agreement has been used. For comparison, Turner (1980, p. 179) gives a figure of 255,118 acres. The temporal pattern in this case is not markedly different from that of the individual acts (see fig. 31).

Precisely how much of each type of land was involved must again be a matter of estimation. Neither Ellis nor Sandell gives a complete break-down, and the sheer size and numbers of awards made sampling, rather than a complete cover, inevitable. The National Enclosure Project ten per cent sample produced figures of 42.15 per cent open field, 3.30 per cent meadow and 44.32 per cent pasture and waste, with the remaining 10.23 per cent representing either old enclosed land which was being exchanged or 'intermixed lands' of dubious status. Wiltshire thus differs from the other three counties in that the areas of common and waste and of open arable involved in parliamentary enclosure are effectively equal; the sampling error is such that the difference between the two cannot be regarded as statistically reliable. Once more, therefore, it emerges as closer to the Midland pattern than any of the others, though far below the percentage of open field in Leicestershire or Northamptonshire (see Chapman, 1987).

Expressed in terms of the Enclosure Index, 197, or over 68 per cent, of the 288 open field systems existing in 1700 were subject to parliamentary action, as were 114, or 79 per cent, of the 144 common meads. For commons and wastes this figure is less meaningful, but the total of 216 (almost $74\frac{1}{2}$ per cent) of the 290 serves to

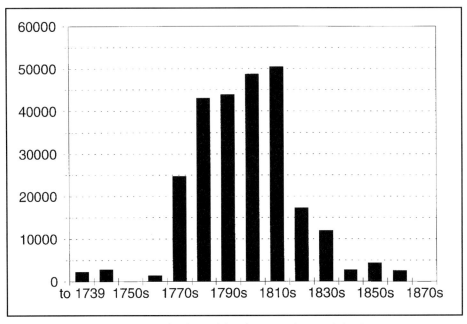

31. Acreages enclosed in Wiltshire by act or order in each decade.

emphasise once again the significance of parliamentary enclosure, as against other means, in Wiltshire.

The large quantity of old enclosed land involved again reflects the peculiar nature of the county's history. As Wiltshire seems to have been particularly prone to use acts to confirm agreements, so it also seems to have used them to an exceptional degree to confirm exchanges of land already enclosed. In view of the rather confused series of partial enclosures which often preceded a parliamentary example in the county, it was inevitable that fragmented patterns of old enclosures had arisen. When an act became necessary to complete the enclosure, it offered the opportunity to redistribute these in a more logical fashion. There is ample evidence that this possibility had formed part of the preliminary discussions, and some allotments are specifically labelled 'to be later exchange for', and laid out to form a compact block for the new owner. Whether this is also the reason why Wiltshire acts often specify that old enclosures of long standing shall be incorporated is not clear. A twenty-year period, such as was imposed at Heddington, Minety and Wootton Bassett, was quite normal elsewhere, but the sixty years at Durnford was most unusual.

Wiltshire seems to have followed the normal pattern in that the earlier phase of the parliamentary movement was weighted towards open fields and the later to common and waste. Most eighteenth century acts dealt with both, though a handful, for example Badbury and Patney, dealt purely with field land. In contrast, a substantial number of nineteenth century acts and orders were concerned solely with common and waste, for example North Bradley and the second Bower Chalke enclosure.

Bower Chalke was something of an oddity amongst parliamentary enclosures, in that the first parliamentary enclosure, under the act of 1785, actually produced a new group of open fields. Examples of enclosures creating new smaller commons out of the land being enclosed are not unusual, and cases occur of commons or even fields being excluded from their scope. However, the Bower Chalke award specifically created a new field system for the copyhold tenants of Chalke manor and, it would appear, included in the arrangement tenants of Stoke Farthing, who had previously had an independent system of their own.[17] Whether this strange arrangement was brought about by a need to defuse opposition from the copyholders, was merely a friendly gesture to meet their wishes, or arose from some more obscure local cause, is unclear. It was certainly highly unusual, and served to prolong open fields in the parish at least into the 1830s after which they seem to have faded away in informal arrangements. They were gone by 1842.[18]

As was discussed earlier, there is no reason to assume that the use of an act was, of necessity, due to opposition, but there is ample evidence that opposition did occur. Michael Turner records 56 failed bills in the county, apparently representing attempts to enclose 42 different areas, of which eight never ultimately had a formal enclosure. Additionally, 13 successful bills faced formal opposition in Parliament.[19] There were five unsuccessful attempts to enclose at Bishopstone, beginning with a bill of 1797, before an act was finally passed in 1809, and then only in the face of two counter-petitions.[20] The rental and survey book of Beechingstoke records an example of the sort of pressure which might be used against opponents in an effort to dissuade them from registering formal objections. A note of 1787 states that only one individual, Thomas Sa(w)yer, was against the proposal to divide the common field, and that his estate should not be renewed 'while he continues this opposition'. The threat appears to have been sufficient, since a further note of 1789 records that he had then consented.[21] An act was passed in the same year, covering Beechingstoke and Urchfont. It may be noted that Sawyer was not some smallholder or minor tenant. He is recorded in 1798 as being in possession of four copyholds totalling over 102 acres, a substantial holding at the time.

Precisely why so many Wiltshire enclosures took such a long time to complete once an act had been passed is not clear, but it is obvious in some cases that the dilatory attitude of the landowners was a factor. At Downton, for example, one of the commissioners, George Barnes, died in 1832. According to the terms of the act, the proprietors should have held a meeting within sixty days to elect a replacement, but in fact no such meeting was ever called. Responsibility for replacing Barnes should then have devolved upon his surviving colleague, Richard Webb, but he in turn took no action, and eventually died five years later without making an appointment. It took a further two years, to 1839, for the proprietors to finally replace Barnes with Frederick James Kelsey. Meanwhile, the Bishop of Winchester, as lord of the manor, should have replaced his nominee, Webb, but he failed to do so until 1845, when he named Francis Attwood. In other words, the enclosure was stalled for 13 years because those who had instigated the enclosure proceedings were not sufficiently concerned to ensure a speedy nomination of new officials.[22]

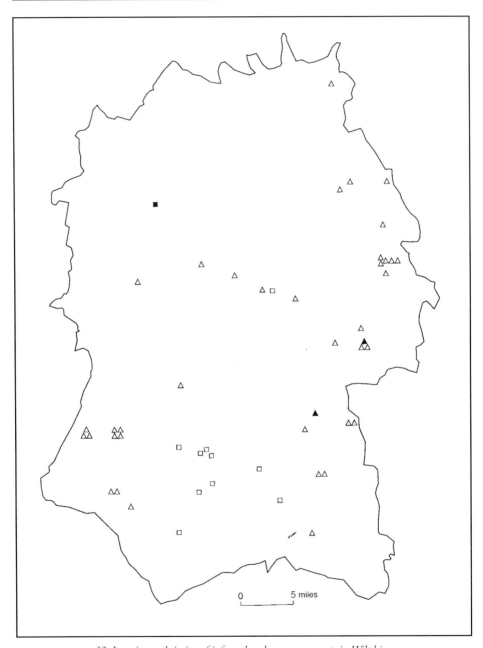

32. Location and timing of informal enclosure agreements in Wiltshire.

In the matter of commissioners, Wiltshire was, once again, closer to the Midland pattern than the other southern counties, for much of the process involved at least one of a limited group of highly experienced local individuals. No less than eight individuals acted ten or more times, against four in Hampshire, and the most prolific, Richard Richardson, was involved in 49, more than double the highest Hampshire total. Richardson was the son of a Darlington-based commissioner, and had gained experience as a surveyor to his father before moving south to Wiltshire in 1778. He subsequently moved to Bath and then London, but operated primarily in Wiltshire and the surrounding counties, acting as commissioner for parliamentary awards at least 71 times, apart from his work as 'umpire' and on private agreements. His awards in Wiltshire represented over 27 per cent of the total for the county, and over 42 per cent of those carried out during his working life. Also highly active was John Gale of Stert, with 25 awards, while George Barnes and Richard Bloxham were significant figures both here and in Hampshire. The occasional stray commissioner from far beyond the county's boundaries can usually be traced to the influence of a particular party, often an institutional owner. The appearance of Joseph Butler of York as a commissioner at Bremhill, together with Joseph and William Dickinson of Beverley as surveyors, was apparently due to the involvement of a landowner with Yorkshire interests who wished to be represented by highly experienced individuals who were well-known to him.

As in the other counties, formal challenges to the decisions of the commissioners were rare, and no Wiltshire award was completely overthrown. Disgruntled individuals complained and issued threats of action, but rarely followed these through. At North Bradley in 1807, for example, Joshua Smith, as Lord of Edington and Rumsey, announced an intention to take legal action against objectors to his claim for common right, which the commissioners had disallowed, but failed to do so within the specified time limit.[23] He did, however, bring an action in the King's Bench in 1814 over the Steeple Ashton enclosure, and won his case, being awarded half of his claim and 1/- damages (Sandell, p.18).

Formal Agreements

The complexity of the enclosure process is reflected in the complexity of the formal agreements. There are a substantial number which specifically state that they are for the 'enclosure' of an area, but where careful reading of the full text casts doubt on precisely what they were really intended to do. Several make provision for the redistribution of lands in the open fields, but leave them subject to either communally controlled cropping patterns or grazing rights after harvest, or both. Such arrangements are hardly enclosures in the normally accepted meaning of the word. Still more confusingly, many appear to involve some element of abolition of rights and controls, whilst retaining them over a part – sometimes the major part – of the area concerned. This not-infrequently applied where there were a number of small manorial tenants, whose lands were consolidated into new open fields, leaving the

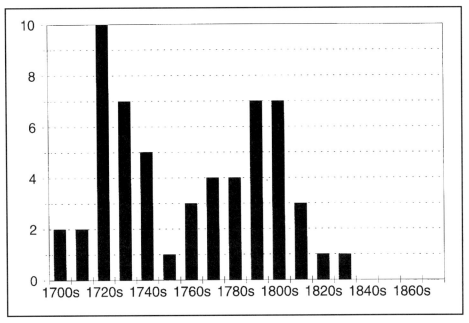

33. Timing of Wiltshire agreements by decade.

larger owners to enclose the rest. Yet other agreements are permissive, retaining the communal system, but allowing any individual to withdraw and fence his land at will. All this variety introduces a certain element of subjectivity into decisions about whether a particular agreement should be regarded as a genuine enclosure. A fairly liberal interpretation has been used in dubious cases, though those which were clearly not enclosures have been excluded from the calculations.

All told, 56 formal agreements were found for the period after 1700, proportionately much the same as for Hampshire and Dorset, though significantly less than for Sussex (see map 32). The *Victoria County History* records others, but it is not always clear whether these meet the definition used here. In some cases a formal agreement seems to have been assumed, while in others, as at Hullavington, the enclosures 'by agreement' were clearly 'informal piecemeal', as defined here (VCH, 14, p113).[24] All these have been rejected, unless there is clear evidence that a formal agreement was concluded. Several agreements have also been omitted since they were subsequently confirmed by an act, thus falling under the definition of 'parliamentary'. Included in this category is the Everley agreement of 1779, though it is not entirely clear that this did indeed refer to the identical area covered by the act. Conversely, a number of other agreements have been counted, even though they refer to the same parish or tithing as an act, since in these cases there seems reasonable doubt as to whether the land involved is the same. As will be discussed later, a good many agreements were partial, leaving parts of individual fields or commons still in communal use, so the fact that the same names reappear is not necessarily evidence that an act is simply confirming an existing enclosure.

Agreements, of course, were not always implemented, and those where there is good evidence of non-completion have also been excluded. The Victoria County History records that the Kennett agreement of 1713 was never followed through (VCH, xii, p.132), and two of those for Longbridge Deverill are specifically endorsed to this effect. The one for 1756 is marked 'Not carried into execution till after a new agreement some years after and then only the fields', and that of 1776 'Never carried into execution on account of Mrs Rogers's not agreeing to it'. The East Commons, incidentally, were included in both. The 1776 agreement clearly deserves to be excluded, and might perhaps be equated with an abortive bill, though it is worth noting that some of the acts which were passed, and which appear in the standard lists of enclosures, were apparently never put into effect. The 1756 case is more difficult, since the implication is that, though it was delayed, a part was ultimately carried out in conjunction with a later agreement. Whether this modified, added to, or superseded the original is unclear. A decision was taken to omit it.[25]

Of the 56 finally accepted, 35 contain acreage figures either in the initial agreement or in the award, where such exists. These 35 give a total figure of just over 15,000 acres. The use of Ellis's figures allows a further three to be estimated, giving just over 18,300 acres. A simple multiplier to account for the missing acreages would therefore imply a total of approximately 27,000 acres enclosed by formal agreement. Though this can be no more than an approximation, there is every reason to suppose that it is of the right order of magnitude, and that the area enclosed by formal agreements, as defined here, amounted to about ten and a half per cent of the parliamentary acreage. The bulk of these agreements tended to be earlier than in the other counties, as can be seen from Figure 7.6 (opposite).

27 post-1700 agreements have sufficient information to allow an accurate picture of the different types of land involved, and this reveals significant differences from the parliamentary movement (see fig. 34). Enclosure by agreement was heavily dominated by open field. 59 per cent of the land dealt with by these agreements was field land, as opposed to only 32 per cent of pasture, waste and down. Old enclosures which were reallocated made up only seven per cent, and common meadow a mere two.

Some indication of the relative importance of formal agreements in dealing with different types of land can be gained by following the procedure used for acts, and calculating the Enclosure Index. In this case 32 (11 per cent) of the fields went in this way, 11 (7.6 per cent) of the meadows, and 31 (10.6 per cent) of the commons. The comparative insignificance of this method in all cases is clear. There are, however, some interesting differences in temporal pattern. While both field and common show an almost 2 to 1 dominance of the eighteenth century,[26] there were six agreements relating to common meadow in the nineteenth as opposed to only 5 in the eighteenth. This difference is emphasised still further when it is realised that all the eighteenth century meadow agreements fell in the 1790s. A possible implication of this is that meadow was of too great an importance to many farmers

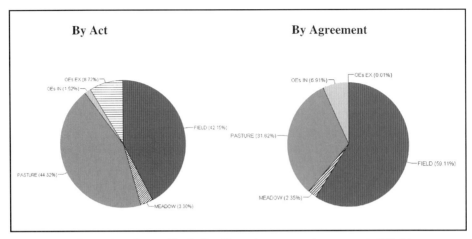

34. Comparison of types of land affected by enclosure acts and agreements in Wiltshire.

in the eighteenth century for agreement to be possible until the very different conditions of the final decade.

As with the other counties, and indeed with enclosures by act, the final agreement might be preceded by a long period of informal exchange and consolidation. The Victoria County History records the gradual accumulation of the various tenancies in Fisherton Delamere and Bapton by the Davis family over the 90 years from 1740 to 1830. By the time of the 1807 agreement for Fisherton, there were only three allottees apart from the Davises, and at the Bapton agreement of 1810 there were only two, which, as the History notes, made the conclusion of the agreements an uncomplicated process (VCH, 8, pp. 41-3). This is not to imply that agreements necessarily involved only a small number of individuals. Of the 28 agreements[27] giving full allotment details, exactly half had ten or more allottees. The Longbridge Deverill agreement of 1778 had only one, but this is misleading. There were in fact 12 parties concerned, but 11 agreed to Viscount Weymouth enclosing part of the common, on condition that he paid the annual value of the land to the Overseers of the Poor to offset the poor rate each year.[28]

One of the characteristic features of Wiltshire agreements is the number which apply to the same parish. Though one or two examples occur in the other three counties, Wiltshire seems to have been particularly prone to this phenomenon, for no reason which is immediately apparent. The most striking case was the Longbridge Deverill one just mentioned, where no less than six separate agreements were concluded, though it appears that only four of these were implemented. The driving force behind this was the Weymouth estate, which seems to have been quite willing to eliminate particular commons one at a time. Such a policy may well have been forced upon them by opposition, though whether this was sufficiently numerous or powerful to have prevented an act, had one been sought, is not clear. However, for whatever reason, the estate pursued this long-drawn-out method rather than seeking alternatives, not merely at Longbridge but also at Horningsham.

The less-wide-ranging nature of some agreement enclosures can be illustrated from Winterbourne Dauntsey. On the 2nd February 1735 five parties agreed to enclose 'the lower part' of North and South Fields, and the Hook Land, a total of just under 43 acres. They further agreed to break up $27\frac{1}{2}$ acres of the Common Down to add to the field land, presumably in replacement of the 43 acres agreed to be enclosed. A year later, the same five parties concluded a second agreement in almost identical terms. This time, just over 15 acres of the lower part of South field were to be enclosed, with 12 acres 122 '*luggs*' (a local term for perch) of down to be taken in compensation. However, open fields survived in the parish until 1851, when 438 acres of North, South, and Little Fields were finally enclosed, under an Order of 1848.[29]

Precisely why such a piecemeal approach to enclosure was adopted is not clear. It is entirely possible that the particular area was chosen for enclosure because it allowed the five to consolidate this with already-enclosed parts of their holdings, though why they failed to include the extra 15 acres in the first place cannot be determined. One can only speculate that caution on the part of one or more of the participants may have persuaded them to start with a small area, and that that had been sufficiently successful for them to add the extra. If it were so instantly successful, it might at first appear strange that the remaining fields survived for another century, but it must be remembered that those with interests in the remainder may have had very different private agendas than did the initial five in the 1730s.

Most agreements make no provision whatever for any change in the tithe arrangements, and payments continued as before. An exception is the agreement for West Overton in 1802, where the Earl of Pembroke and the Duke of Marlborough each owned various types of tithes on the same pieces of land. As part of the general enclosure of the open land and a redistribution of scattered old-enclosed plots, the two agreed to exchange tithes, so that each allotment owed tithes to only one of them.

The surviving documentation for enclosure agreements tends to be sparse, so the Cholderton case in 1737 is of particular interest, since papers covering some of the negotiations prior to the agreement survive.[30] The aim was to enclose the Sheep Down, an area of just under 220 acres which was being used for pasture for 560 sheep, and there were four parties, three right owners and the lord of the manor, one William Kingsmill. The evidence survives because Kingsmill had been declared a lunatic, and management of his estate handed over by the High Court to Hugh Corry, a London lawyer, necessitating an exchange of letters between Corry and the other parties. These reveal that Henry Hoare, by far the minority owner with less than four acres ultimately allotted, initially insisted on a clause preventing Corry from enclosing the manorial allotment, while Corry raised objections about the status of a tenant-for-life under a settlement. Hoare was eventually persuaded to withdraw the clause, and John Lee Hill put up a bond of £500 to indemnify Corry should anyone subsequently lay claim to Hill's allotment. He also agreed to pay Corry's share of the costs of surveying the down. The agreement was then able to go ahead without any use of independent commissioners or referees.

It is clear from the correspondence that the initiative for this enclosure came from the right owners, rather than the lord, and it is also clear that they were anxious to complete it as quickly as possible, in order to move ahead with projected improvements. Lee Hill included a comment that he hoped the deeds to the new allotments would arrive 'before the season for burnbaking is over',[31] indicating his desire to begin the reclamation process immediately. The fact that he was willing both to put up a very substantial bond and pay the lord's expenses strengthens the view that he and Anthony Cracherode were the prime movers.

The problems and frustrations of using formal agreements can be illustrated from West Knoyle.[32] Henry Hoare, lord of the manor (and apparently the same individual as the party at Cholderton) began the process in 1741 by concluding a bilateral agreement with a customary tenant, Nathaniel Hickman. The terms were that Hickman should surrender his general *levant* and *couchant* rights on the commons in exchange for the right to enclose 12 acres of Gonmoor Hill, and should be given a new lease at a cost of £40. An agreement was then concluded in 1742 with all the customary tenants to enclose Westhill Common (containing 200 acres), and in 1743 it was further agreed at the Court Baron that the 76-acre Old Common which was 'very much incumbered with thorns', and therefore worth very little to the commoners, should be enclosed and placed under the control of trustees who would let it to support the poor of the parish.

Having achieved his enclosure, Hoare then became involved in two separate disputes. In the first, the vicar, the Revd William Barford, wrote to Hoare complaining that he had not been informed of the enclosure beforehand, that his allotment was by general consent not worth enclosing, and that he had been given no beastgates on that part of the common which was to be left open. Richard Willoughby, formerly Hoare's steward, and a substantial landholder in his own right, responded with a letter openly contemptuous of Barford, who, he alleged, was avoiding his duties by foisting 'a little coxcomb' on the parish as curate, and who he described as suffering from 'insatiable avarice'. As Willoughby pointed out, mere possession of land did not imply possession of common rights, and he himself held land to which none were attached. The parson's cows had previously been impounded for trespass, showing that his claim was invalid, and he was simply attempting to take advantage of the situation. Hoare was obviously irritated by Willoughby's role in the matter, and appears to have suspected him of sharp practice, for there is a mention of 'Old Cary's' opinion that Hoare himself had lost out due to a misrepresentation of the beastgates upon which the shares were based. The dispute appears to have been allowed to drop, but had Barford pursued it he could probably have had the agreement overthrown, on the grounds that it had been imposed without his knowledge and consent. An act would have protected Hoare from these problems.

The second dispute arose from the death of Hickman shortly after the agreement. It had been discovered that his twelve acres on Gonmoor Hill in fact amounted to only 7 acres 3 roods and 30 perches, and Hickman had complained to the referees for the Westhill enclosure, who had allotted him a further 10 acres and 28 perches. Hoare appears to have taken this to mean that the first agreement was void, while Mrs Mitchell, Hickman's heiress, maintained that he should be compelled to offer a lease for £40 for the life of her son and heir, John, since Hickman had not taken up the agreed lease before his death. Mrs Mitchell threatened a bill in the Court of Chancery to force Hoare to comply. Willoughby acted as go-between, advising Mrs Mitchell not to plunge into an expensive lawsuit, and Hoare to grant the lease, implying that Hoare would lose if the matter came to court. Again, the matter appears to have been resolved privately, but again the terms of a parliamentary award would almost certainly have avoided such a dispute.

As a final comment, Wiltshire offers the only example found in these counties of an intermediate stage between the formal and informal enclosures, albeit strictly speaking outside the time-limits of this volume. The Ludgershall agreement of 1682 was a formal written document agreed by all the parties involved, but it was effectively a formalisation of a piecemeal enclosure, for the parties merely agreed to fence off their separate pieces of land as then held, in other words without any apparent reorganisation. However, it is clear from the document that some form of consolidation and simplification of ownership had already taken place, since some of the lands concerned are recorded as having been purchased from other landowners. Characteristically, most of these sellers were absentee owners, living outside the county.[33]

Informal Enclosure

Informal enclosure seems to have been a much less complete process in Wiltshire than in the other counties in that far fewer whole systems were eliminated in this way after 1700. The evidence suggests that, while many systems were quite extensively encroached, there was usually some formal end-point, which might, or might not, incorporate some or all of the already informally enclosed land; as a consequence the crude Index is more than usually misleading, and must represent a significant understatement. Amongst the fields, only 58 systems were expunged without any formal procedure, though parts of the Wilcot system seem to have continued after the agreement of 1730, and the newly created fields resulting from the Broad Chalke act ultimately vanished without formality. Both the meadows and commons were apparently proportionately even less affected: only $12\frac{1}{2}$ per cent of the former and just under 15 per cent of the latter disappeared wholly by this means.

Calculating any correction to the Enclosure Index is complicated by the apparent differential understatement of the different land types. Ellis offers some estimates of losses by parish, but only for a limited time span, and he does not distinguish between the types of land in these figures. As always, it was the commons which seem to have suffered the greatest levels of loss prior to any formal enclosure of the parish, though there is ample evidence of the fields also being reduced. At Alvediston much of the down was ploughed up in 1758, leaving the North Down to parliamentary action in 1792, and at Chilmark 100 acres was taken in in 1793, though a final enclosure was not completed until the act of 1861. As for fields, Fisherton Anger had land removed only six years before the parliamentary enclosure (VCH, vi, pp. 186-8). Common meadows seem to have been less liable to this process, though examples exist. There is evidence of much early enclosure of the meadows of Hankerton (VCH, xiv, pp. 99-100), but parts of Strait Meadow were included in the act of 1808.

No particular spatial or temporal pattern seems to be discernible. The informal disappearance of the more easily detectable fields was spread over the whole period from 1700 to the second half of the nineteenth century, with one, Stert, surviving well into the twentieth. As far as can be ascertained, 36 were lost in the eighteenth century and 22 in the nineteenth,[34] indicating a slightly earlier bias than parliamentary enclosures, but not one of great significance.

Spatially, informal enclosures were widely scattered about the county, though with small groupings in certain areas, for example in the vicinities of Trowbridge and Devizes. Urban influences may have played some small part, since disintegration in the presence of local markets is evidenced elsewhere, and local example and know-how must have encouraged imitation. Ultimately, however, the pattern seems to represent nothing much more than the chance occurrence, in some parishes, of circumstances which allowed either the lord to consolidate or other individuals to withdraw land without opposition.

Wiltshire has examples of all the variations on informal enclosures shown by the other counties, but again not in the same proportions. Consolidation at landowner level seems to have been far more significant than by tenant. One of the few cases of the latter seems to have been at Highway, where the fact that the location of the glebe was unknown in 1677 points to a tenant enclosure under way there, though parts of the system were nominally still open in 1841.[35] On the other hand, examples of consolidation by landowners abound. In Throope manor, all the arable was accumulated into a single farm by 1708, while at Little Langford the owner managed to combine everything except the glebe into a single farm by the latter years of the eighteenth century, a subsequent exchange with the rector consolidating the ownership pattern (VCH, XV, p. 180). Boscombe remained theoretically in common husbandry until enclosed by an Order of 1862,[36] but was effectively almost entirely consolidated into one farm well before.

Piecemeal consolidation by the major landowner can be illustrated from Huish, which was owned in the late eighteenth century by the trustees of Froxfield Hospital. In 1773 a decision was taken not to renew copyholds when they fell due, and the trustees were thus able gradually to amalgamate these with Huish Farm. They apparently took advantage of the Oare enclosure of 1803 to complete the consolidation by confirming exchanges with the rector and another owner. Thus some 390 acres, 175 of the open field and 215 down and wood, ceased to be common (VCH, 10, pp.79-80).

The messy process which characterised so many enclosures can be seen from the neighbouring parishes of Fonthill Bishop and Fonthill Gifford. In the former, some enclosure had apparently taken place between 1700 and 1744, and there was an agreement to enclose more of the open fields about 1760. What remained was gradually accumulated into the hands of one individual, William Beckford finally acquiring the last tenantry land in 1796. Once more, characteristically, he was left with the problem of the church land, and an exchange with the rector was necessary to complete the process (VCH, 8, pp.79-80). Fonthill Gifford followed the same lines, with most of the open field land falling into a single farm by 1754, though William Beckford again played the final decisive role by buying up all the remaining open land and rights between 1787 and 1818 (VCH, 8, 163-4).

Summary

By comparison with the other three counties, Wiltshire's enclosure history appears relatively conventional. Almost 30 per cent of its area was affected by parliamentary enclosure, while the other means added of the order of another 11 per cent, a clear minority. It seems likely that less than 41 per cent of the county was affected overall. Furthermore, formal agreements made up a far more significant proportion of the non-parliamentary share. Though it accounted for a good deal less than informal methods, the discrepancy was far less than in the others – something of the order of $4\frac{1}{4}$ per cent of the county as against $6\frac{3}{4}$ per cent. Even allowing for a probable under-recording of the latter, due to Wiltshire's tendency to include already-enclosed land in parliamentary enclosures, there is still a significant difference.

However, though at first glance Wiltshire's enclosure pattern bears a close resemblance to the standard Midland one, the foregoing discussion has highlighted major differences. The amount of non-parliamentary enclosure during the two centuries was far higher than the classical Midland pattern, in spite of the large number of acts and orders. Furthermore, the parliamentary movement itself was more complex and confusing than was normal in the Midland counties, and was operating on a more complex and fluid system. All the evidence points to the Wiltshire communal agricultural system having a far greater flexibility in the distinction between arable and pasture than, say, Leicestershire, and the multiplicity of separate systems within a single parish also distinguishes it. The fact that systems seem to have frequently separated and merged adds confusion to the enclosure history, as does the un-Midland habit of enclosing several parishes under a single act. In many ways, therefore, Wiltshire emerges as intermediate in its enclosure history between the traditional Midland pattern and that discussed earlier for the other three counties. Given its geographical location, this is perhaps not surprising, but it serves to emphasise once more the degree of spatial variation to be found within the process.

8

Conclusion

A key question which remains is the impact of the wave of enclosure, which has been discussed in the preceding chapters. How far did it actually alter the landscape and environment, the farming system, and rural society of these counties? A great deal has been written, especially about the last of these, but much of this is based on the premise that enclosure, at least from 1750 onwards, can be equated with parliamentary enclosure, a premise which the foregoing discussion has shown to be untenable. Comments on the farming system have tended to proceed from the same starting point, as have the relatively limited references to landscape and environment. A re-examination of these topics therefore seems appropriate.

The farming system

If we begin with the farming system, which, after all, was what enclosure was intended to change, it is obvious that the different methods of enclosure would be likely to produce different outcomes. The traditional picture of a system of block farms emerging from a chaos of small scattered strips is an over-simplification even for the 'classic' parliamentary enclosure, where virtually the whole parish – fields, meadows, and commons – was converted at a stroke: most such enclosures produced ownership patterns broken into two or three discrete blocks. Where parliamentary enclosures were concerned with commons, as many in these southern counties were, they were apt to increase the degree of fragmentation, since many allottees had no land immediately adjoining the common to which their new allotments could be attached. Single-block farms were most likely to occur where one or two major landowners received very large allotments which could then be divided up into viable farms for letting, and there is certainly evidence of this, most notably on the newly enclosed downlands of Wiltshire, Hampshire and, to a lesser extent, Dorset. For most small to medium landowners, their new holdings, and hence any owner-occupied farms, would still show some fragmentation, and they might well have acquired one or more tiny scraps of inconveniently situated former common. Nevertheless, parliamentary enclosure normally produced ownership units which were very markedly more efficient than those which preceded them.

The dominance of other methods of enclosure over Sussex and substantial parts of Hampshire and Dorset implies rather different results. The fact that formal agreements so frequently involved only one particular part of a parish – a single common, or even one field – meant that even the imperfect level of consolidation achieved by the parliamentary method was not possible. Since it was so often commons which were involved, fragmentation almost inevitably increased. In parts of Sussex and Dorset where farm consolidation had long been achieved (if fragmentation had ever existed), the effect was to *produce* fragmentation. Again, because of the nature of the agreements, many fragmented pieces were very small. For many farmers the price to pay for a cheaper means of enclosure was a less efficient one.

Informal enclosures produced by far the greatest variation. As has been stressed, *de facto* enclosure by consolidation at tenant level often produced an extremely efficient farm lay-out without any significant consolidation of the ownership pattern. Gradual alteration to ownership, by sale or exchange, had no bearing whatsoever on farm lay-out. On the other hand, informal piecemeal enclosure, whereby owners fenced off strips in the fields or small pieces of the common, often fossilised a high degree of fragmentation in the case of fields, or increased it in that of commons. In the fields, much depended on the extent to which adjacent strips were already in the same ownership by 1700. Significant consolidation was already present in some parishes by that date, and 'piecemeal' enclosure here might result in quite large blocks, rarely anything as efficient as parliamentary enclosure was able to achieve, but nevertheless enough to allow the creation of fields of a viable size. More characteristically, however, a mere handful of strips might be amalgamated and enclosed, leaving very tiny field units which tended to be highly persistent (see fig 35). While the value of such tiny units was limited from the agricultural point of view, they were often well suited for the development of close-packed urban housing, and the process left its mark on the structure of a number of southern towns, notably Portsmouth and Brighton.

Rural society

Though detailed investigation of the social impact of enclosure is beyond the remit of this book, the conclusions outlined have obvious implications for the debates on social outcomes. One hotly disputed question, for example, has been the extent to which enclosure was a major contributing factor to the decline in the peasant/yeoman/small owner-occupier. Much of the evidence presented on both sides has been concerned with the extent to which small owners sold their land after enclosure, and how far the level of sales was an unusual feature triggered by the costs of enclosure. If, however, much consolidation of the plots in the open fields was actually achieved by substantial tenants renting land from a variety of small owners, as the evidence from these southern counties suggests, the nature of the debate is changed. The fact that small *landowners* sold land is no evidence that small *farmers* were going out of business at that particular moment; they might have ceased to farm

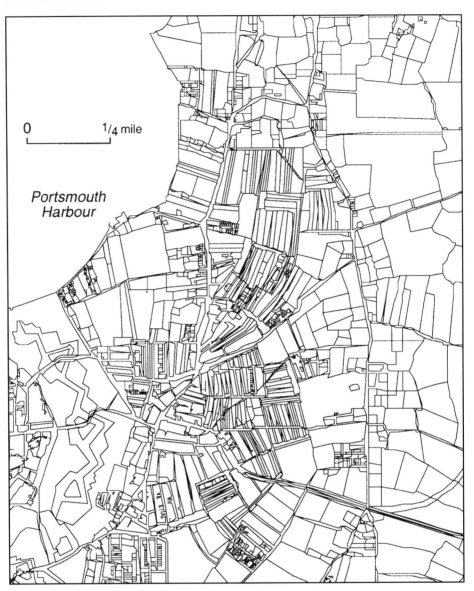

35. Effects of piecemeal enclosure on Portsea Island. Contrast the small, narrow strips of the informally enclosed central and north western part of the island with the larger and broader fields of the formally enclosed eastern part of the map.

long before. The Sussex evidence certainly supports the idea that the small owners who were selling at enclosure had occupations other than farming and/or were absentees. They were not small peasant proprietors driven from their farming occupation by the costs of enclosure. Enclosure may well have been the trigger for many, but only because keeping an eye on a distant small plot may have seemed more trouble than the rent was worth, and the upheaval of a formal enclosure would be an appropriate incentive to sell up. Conversely, evidence that large estates were buying up land at enclosure is not necessarily evidence that farm units became larger at that moment. If the tenant was already renting the land from the selling owner, there might be no change whatsoever at the practical farming level. This is not to suggest that no change took place, only that it is very easy to exaggerate its extent, or misunderstand its nature.

The evidence of the large proportion of informal and agreement enclosure also has significant implications. Large landowners could, and on occasions undoubtedly did, put heavy pressure on their weaker neighbours to accept an agreement, and there were certainly cases where the lord acted arbitrarily and without regard for the claimed rights of others. Nevertheless, for the most part enclosures by agreement resulted in relatively good terms for the smaller owners, including the cottagers with rights. Cases where the lord or a major landowner covered all their expenses were not infrequent, and the small owners were sometimes allotted a single block between them, giving them a choice as to when they wished to split off their own individual portion. Even the fencing costs could thus be delayed until they felt it convenient. If they did have to meet some or all of the costs, an agreement was almost certain to be a much cheaper procedure than an act, and they were in a position to negotiate the conditions which seemed significant to them, rather than being reliant on the arbitration of an outsider, who would be guided by strict legal niceties and precedents. Even those who had no legal rights might gain something from an agreement, as at Longbridge Deverill where they were to be permitted to buy such quantity as should be 'needful for them'. From the point of view of the major landowners, offering relatively generous terms was clearly in their interests, since they avoided not only the extra expenses but also the delays of the parliamentary procedure, and probably minimised the possibilities of physical attacks on the fences as well.

Informal enclosures of fields in theory placed no burden at all upon the small owners. They might be at some disadvantage in terms of their ability to keep stock on the isolated strips, but they were not forced to incur any expenditure at all. As has been stated, many of them in fact gave up farming at some point, renting their lands out to others, such that they were never involved in any 'enclosure' in the normal sense of the word. Some even had no idea which were their lands, the tenant presumably merely paying rent for the appropriate number of acres to each individual who owned part of his farm. Until they wished to realise the value of that land there was no reason for the owners to be concerned, and no doubt they often eventually sold to one of the other owners or the tenant. Precisely when such a field could be said to be no longer open is a matter of semantics.

As for informal enclosures of commons, a distinction must be made between the effects of gradual encroachment on a common, as happened at Horsham, and the gradual accumulation of rights into the hands of one individual, as happened on Brighton down. While the former might prove a significant burden, since the area available to any small farmer attempting to run stock would be increasingly restricted, and rights such as fuel gathering would eventually disappear, the latter would not affect him until the moment when he chose to leave. There is ample evidence that in practice many individuals simply ceased to use their rights, or leased or sold them to one or two individuals who gradually consolidated them, so that it was the number of right holders which diminished, not the size of the common. That only vanished when all rights were in the hands of one individual, or the two or three remaining holders finally split the land. These last few individuals were rarely active small farmers.

It must also be remembered that many of the southern commons were large, so even gradual encroachment upon them often had little immediate impact. Again, this is not to suggest that there was no effect, for quite clearly there was, but the evidence of problems and hostile reactions in some places cannot be taken as evidence that the problems were felt elsewhere.

A further issue which has been the subject of much comment is the question of relationship between the amount of land received by each owner after enclosure and that which they had before. A number of writers, for example Cohen and Weitzman (1975, p. 163) and Neeson (1989, p. 98), have assumed that the amount received must be less, due to the deductions of land to compensate the tithe owners. This assumption has then formed the basis of an argument that owners with holdings which were just viable before enclosure were pushed into non-viability as a consequence, and were forced out of farming. However, even if we focus purely on those owners who were still actively farming, the results for the southern counties cast serious doubts on this argument.

Firstly, it is clear that even parliamentary enclosures frequently did not compensate for tithes; owners continued to pay in kind as before, so there was no such deduction. For non-parliamentary enclosures, this situation held even more strongly; it was rare for tithes to be abolished in exchange for land. Additionally, as has been pointed out, a significant proportion of both the parliamentary and non-parliamentary enclosure in these counties, especially Dorset and Sussex, took place after the Tithe Commutation Act, which removed the tithe from the equation. For a great many owners, therefore, the tithe question was an irrelevance.

Secondly, since a very substantial majority of the land concerned was former common and waste, rather than field land, the 'average' landowner actually received more land than he had had before, even if land *was* taken to compensate for tithes. True, he had lost his share of the common grazing, but the actual size of his personal holding was increased. Again, this is not to suggest that small landowners never ended up with less land, for there was no such thing as an average enclosure. What does emerge, is that in the southern counties landowners were more likely to be allotted larger holdings at enclosure than they had had before, and any argument that holdings were generally reduced cannot be sustained.

The Landscape and Environment

The description 'Enclosure Landscape' has found its way not merely into the specialist works on agricultural and landscape history, but also into a much wider literature aimed at the general public. It evokes an image of large rectangular fields with neat hedges – the 'Georgian landscape' of Michael Turner. In most parliamentary enclosures hedging, rather than any other form of boundary, was specifically laid down as compulsory: indeed the actual species of hedging plant to be used was frequently specified, the hawthorn being the favoured one because of its speed of growth and its ability to produce a stock-proof barrier. In consequence, such landscapes were widespread in Wiltshire and over significant parts of Hampshire and Dorset and many still remain, though the modern practice of grubbing up hedges has greatly modified and reduced them. Ironically, the much-criticised 'prairie fields' resulting from this grubbing-up have tended to produce something resembling the older pre-enclosure landscapes, with their open, unhedged vistas. However, as the foregoing comments have made clear, this 'Enclosure Landscape' is in fact only *one* of the enclosure landscapes. It is essentially the product of large-scale parliamentary enclosure, which is only a part of the story, for much was non-parliamentary, and even parliamentary enclosure was often small-scale.

Non-parliamentary enclosures could, of course, produce similar landscapes. Where large estates dominated the process, or there were only a couple of landowners involved, it was possible to produce a similar, or even more regular, pattern. The landscapes resulting from the enclosures at Warnford in Hampshire or Burleston in Dorset are indistinguishable from their parliamentary equivalents. Some formal agreements also imposed hedging regulations identical to those of parliamentary ones. However, more frequently the result was a much more compact and less regular pattern. The informal enclosure of Hunston, Sussex, produced a landscape of small hedged fields very different from the traditional picture, though the adjoining parliamentary enclosure, covering a small area with several owners, was not distinguishable from it. As has already been mentioned, the urban landscapes of Portsmouth and Brighton still bear signs of the piecemeal enclosures of the fields on which they were developed, and, in the case of Portsmouth, much more extensive areas remained into the 1960s, when most were swept away by urban redevelopment.

The environmental impacts of these changes have received little attention, but they are certainly worthy of some consideration, especially in the light of the strong environmentalist concerns which emerged in the last years of the twentieth century. The large open fields were inevitably subject to soil erosion on a significant scale, protected only by the inability of eighteenth and nineteenth century farmers to kill off the weeds, which rapidly provided an element of cover to any open land. The bare fallow was particularly vulnerable, especially if local custom involved several ploughings, destroying any covering vegetation. Where, as in much of Dorset, Hampshire, and Wiltshire, these fields lay on the sloping chalklands, the potential for erosion was still further increased. The full effects of this are a matter of continuing debate, but there can be little doubt that the new enclosures represented an improvement. The newly planted hedgerows offered a barrier to soil movement, as can be readily observed from the build-up of material against the uphill side of many existing ones in the region, so that the erosional process was, at the very least, slowed down.

There must also have been significant wildlife implications. The open, unhedged fields prior to enclosure provided an appropriate environment for a particular group of species, the skylark and the corncrake for example, and favoured the hare as against the rabbit. The new hedges and smaller fields, on the other hand, provided nesting sites for a different range, the whitethroat and the blackbird for example, and offered an ideal opportunity for the rabbit, for which the hedges provided both cover and a place to construct burrows. What we have come to accept as the norm in terms of wildlife patterns must have been subtly different three hundred years ago, and must have undergone a gradual process of change as a result of enclosure, regardless of any other influences affecting it.

Against this must be set the effects of enclosure on the commons. Though some of these were over-grazed prior to enclosure, and some may have been locally stripped of turf and other vegetation for fuel, most were covered by a semi-natural vegetation of heath, scrub, or woodland, depending on local physical conditions and the degree of human pressure on their resources. Given their very varied nature, from chalk downlands to acid heaths and broad-leafed woodland, their characteristics were far less uniform than those of the fields, but as a broad generalisation they were relatively well protected from erosion, and offered sanctuary to a far more diverse range of wildlife species.

In both of these respects, enclosure tended to be highly damaging. In so far as attempts were made to reclaim these 'new' lands, this frequently involved the stripping off of the existing vegetation and the conversion of the land into large fields which were much more open to erosional processes. Furthermore, the clearing process most commonly involved paring and burning, i.e. the cutting of the vegetation and its burning *in situ* to create an ash which would give some fertility when ploughed in. Unfortunately this release of fertility was very short-lived, and the evidence is that few of these areas received significant further inputs, at least before the later nineteenth century when improved transport and the availability of 'artificial' fertilizers altered the situation. The other effect of paring and burning was to increase the acidity of the soil, a disaster where acidity was already high. Though lime could be used to counteract this, cost and transport difficulties were often a deterrent. As a consequence, many would-be reclaimers fought a losing battle against a deteriorating environment, as Thomas Hardy's fictional accounts of the Dorset heathlands vividly portray. Much of this land was later abandoned, often in waves as agricultural depression finally tipped the balance against the struggling farmer, but having suffered significant damage in the mean time.

In the longer term, the enclosure of these lands had far greater effects. The fact that they were in private ownership made them a prime target for intensification of use in periods of agricultural expansion and pressure, for example during the two world wars, and the varying systems of grants, price support and subsidies since 1945 have often tipped the balance in favour of ploughing and cropping these areas. The heavy losses of downland and heathland which have occurred in the second half of the twentieth century are, in large measure, of lands which were enclosed after 1700.

From the wildlife point of view, the effect of this elimination of the commons was to reduce a wide variety of different habitats, woodland, heathland and downland, to the same limited range provided by the former fields. Initially, a small group of species must have benefited by the change, annual plants adapted to newly disturbed ground, such as the poppy, and field-nesting birds, such as the skylark. In the longer term, these in turn have fallen victim to herbicides, earlier grass-cutting, combine harvesting, and other twentieth century agricultural practices. For the great majority of plant and animal species, the last refuge when the commons had gone was the new hedgerows created by the same process. Thus two of the major environmental issues in southern England at the end of the twentieth century owe much, in different ways, to the enclosure movements of the two previous centuries. The responsibility for the precarious existence of such dwindling habitats as the Dorset heaths or the Sussex downs must ultimately rest with the effectiveness of that enclosure. In contrast, it is to those same movements that we owe so many of the hedgerows which are much prized today for their contribution to the landscape and much valued for their role in maintaining some remnants of the former wildlife of the region.

General Implications

This study has been based entirely on four counties in central southern England, and, as the continuing work of the National Enclosure Project has already demonstrated, many aspects of enclosure were subject to great variations from one part of the country to another. It would therefore be quite inappropriate to assume that the conclusions reached for these counties necessarily apply elsewhere. However, it does raise the question as to whether some other areas might follow a similar pattern, and, if so, how extensive such areas might be. Preliminary investigations elsewhere certainly confirm that non-parliamentary enclosure was a normal feature of the eighteenth and nineteenth centuries in several counties outside the Midland belt, and that the processes discussed here were by no means unique to these southern counties. Hertfordshire, for example, shows a high degree of informal enclosure, and strong evidence of 'tenant enclosure', stretching not merely through the nineteenth century, but even into the twentieth. It seems most unlikely, therefore, that the picture presented by these southern counties is totally unique to that area. At the very least it poses serious questions about some of the traditional assumptions about the enclosure movement after 1700.

The myth that enclosure equalled parliamentary enclosure of open fields has long been exploded, though it continues to surface, even in academic discussion of the subject. What is not yet clear is precisely what the norm, if such exists, might be. It would be no surprise if the southern counties ultimately prove closer to the 'average national pattern' than the traditional heartland of enclosure studies.

Notes

1 Introduction

1. See Chapter 2, p. 16-17.
2. Turner records the national figure as 20.9 per cent, Dorset as 15.0, Hampshire as 16.8 and Wiltshire as 29.4, with Leicestershire 46.6 and Northamptonshire 53.0. Revisions to these figures are given in later chapters.

2 The Enclosure Process

1. For a detailed discussion of tithes see Kain and Prince (1985).
3. Corpus Christi Archives Cb 18/6.
4. Land provided for the upkeep of the parish priest.
5. See Appendix I. In addition, Broad Blunsdon and Heddington (Wiltshire) both enclosed new land, but confirmed older enclosures at the same time.
6. 'Raised and resident'.
7. PCRO L2/8/1-4, 1697.
8. WSRO Ep VI/27.
9. 15 & 16 Vic c.51 allowed abolition on demand. Some copyholds persisted into the twentieth century, until formal abolition in 1926.
10. WRO 212B/3732.
11. DRO Inc 92.
12. ESRO Glynde Place 3172.
13. We are very grateful to Professor Turner for making his manuscript lists available to us. A discussion of failed bills is contained in Turner, Michael and Wray, Trevor (1991), 'A Survey of Sources for Parliamentary Enclosure: the House of Commons Journal and Commissioners' Working Papers', *Archives*, 19, pp. 257-288.
14. Corpus Christi Archives Cb 18/5.
15. Portsmouth City RO CLC 4/13.
16. WSRO Add Ms 5163.
17. HRO 10M57/A3/11.
18. At Littleton, Hampshire (HRO 49M95/559).
19. See, for example, D. N. Mcloskey 'English Open Fields as Behaviour towards Risk', in P. Uselding, *Research in Economic History*, (London, 1976).
20. HRO 10M57/A3/9 and Q23/2/105.
21. Evidence of George Maxwell, one of the leading commissioners, to Parliamentary Committee in House of Commons Sessional Papers of the Eighteenth Century, Reports and Papers 1799-1800, vol. 130, p. 25.

3 Sources

1. For the effect of the 1801 act, see p. 34.
2. Except where manorial waste was involved.

3. The act estimate is 1500 acres, whereas the allotments total only 1182 acres.
4. House of Commons Journal, 64 (1809), p. 69.
5. House of Commons Journal, 76 (1812), p. 189.
6. Corpus Christi Archives Cb18/5, letter of 26 October 1788.
7. North Yorkshire Record Office PR/TAW5, letter from Lord Ailesbury to his agent.
8. See Chapman, 1980; WSRO Add Mss 5179 and Raper, uncat., Box15.
9. WSRO Add Mss 6004-6008.
10. See p. 32-33.
11. Enclosure 10093. DRO Book iv, p 423.
12. HRO 10M69/E25.
13. Enclosure 10083. DRO D396.
14. For example, at Llangwm, Denbighshire. See Chapman (1992), pp. 81-82.
15. Hampshire Museums Service FA1994.26.
16. WSRO QDD/6/E14.
17. Portsmouth City RO CLC4/13.
18. DRO Fox-Strangeways D/FSI/151.
19. For example, the Oaker Common (Hampshire) award is in the Cornwall Record Office.
20. HRO 8M49/T68.
21. PRO IR29/ and IR30/35/87 and 35/45.
22. 'Ersh' was a local term for stubble.
23. WRO 490/1007.
24. WRO EA 169.
25. For example, at Winterbourne, Dorset, where the stint was reduced from 4 sheep per arable acre to 1 in 1691. DRO D/SHE/1.

4 Dorset

1. Some parishes contained more than one system, so fewer contained systems than might at first appear.
2. D/GLY:B/P3,4 and T/FOM.
3. D/FFO/38/18 and PE/BRA:SC3/4.
4. DRO D/WLC:/E62.
5. See Chapter 3, pp. 45-6.
6. DRO D/BOH:P2.
7. PRO IR29/ and IR30/10/34.
8. DRO Inc 88.
9. DRO Inc 59.
10. There were no copyholders.
11. One of the ten 'owners' was in fact two individuals owning jointly, one of whom, Mary Bird, had some land of her own as well.
12. See Chapter 3, pp. 32-3.
13. 15.04 per cent.
14. 1443.87 acres, by addition.
15. Oddly, the column for enclosures under the 1836 act is left blank, though there were 16 in the

county. The totals add up correctly.

16. 63% containing open field in each case.
17. It did, however, involve exchanges of old enclosures.
18. Endacott gives 39 acres of pasture, but in fact over 38 of these were common meadow, leaving only about half an acre of pasture.
19. DRO KY16/1-38.
20. DRO KY/16/18. At the time of writing this collection was not fully catalogued, and references were liable to alteration.
21. DRO Inc 92.
22. DRO D/RGB/658.
23. DRO QSM 1/13.
24. DRO QSM 1/13.
25. DRO D/FAR/T18.
26. Taylor (1970, p. 128) records one for Broadwinsor in 1677.
27. The Hilton award, however, appears incomplete
28. DRO D/FIL/E5.
29. DRO D/PLR/M8.
30. See p. 47.
31. DRO D148/17/64.
32. DRO D/MAP/E109 and D/PUD/M6.
33. D/BOH:/T14-44.
34. D/BOH:P2.
35. DRO D/FFO/38/18 and PE/BRA:SC3/4.
36. DRO D/PSS/E1.
37. DRO Photocopy 529.

5 *Hampshire*

1. Excluding those which may have disappeared in the Middle Ages.
2. HRO 8M58/22.
3. For example, the agreement enclosure at Wootton St. Lawrence in the 1620s (HRO 21M58/L1-2) and a parliamentary enclosure of the wastes in 1829-32 do not account for the whole acreage of the parish, and of the three separate field systems identified: the Ramsdell system seems to have been enclosed by informal means. North Hayling was subject to seven separate parliamentary enclosures, of both common arable and wastes, and Titchfield had four, all of waste.
4. HRO 10M57/A3/7.
5. HRO Q23/1/134.
6. HRO 10M57/A3/8.
7. WCA T3A/1/3/8, dated December 1821.
8. HRO Q23/1/2, pp. 450-69 text and 21M63/3 map.
9. HRO 109M82/89.
10. HRO 21M61/7, dated 1771.
11. HRO58M71/E/B/11.
12. See HRO Q23/2/113 for text and Copy/319/1 for working maps.
13. Hampshire Telegraph, no. 648, 9th March 1812.
14. CJ 56, p. 201 and 57, p.131.
15. HRO 4M53/250/3.
16. HRO 4M53/250/2.

17. HRO 4M53/250/5.
19. HRO 4M53/250/9.
20. HRO 4M53/250/11. Kent was a former bailiff to George the Third, and had experience as an enclosure Commissioner in Norfolk and Oxfordshire.
21. 'Driver' was Abraham Pursehouse Driver, who was frequently a Crown nominee as an enclosure Commissioner, and who also worked for the Crown as a surveyor in the New Forest.
22. HRO 4M53/250/19.
23. HRO 4M53/250.19.
24. HRO 4M53/250/21.
25. HRO 4M53/250/15.
26. HRO 10M69/E25.
27. HRO 10M69/E26.
28. HRO 10M69/E27.
29. HRO 86M87/14/2.
30. HRO Copy/288/41.
31. HRO Q23/2/86.
32. A reference to the Act for consolidating in one Act certain provisions usually inserted in Acts of Inclosure, 41 Geo. III.
33. HRO 33M49/1, map, probably partly by Isaac Taylor, of land belonging to Joshua Iremonger.
34. HRO 27M92/51.
35. I.e. the right to the pasture of the roads and roadside verges.
36. See HRO 21M58/L1-2 for the full text of the dispute.
37. HRO 44M69/J9/126 (3).
38. HRO 35M48/16/29, which contains the last clear reference to common arable fields in Bighton.
39. HRO 105M88/3.
40. HRO 38M48/159.
41. HRO 4M62/262/1.
42. HRO 50M89/16.
43. HRO 4M62/262/4.
44. *Hampshire Telegraph*, no. 660, 1st June 1812.
45. HRO 12M74/E/T28.
46. HRO 10M54/108.
47. Although they are mentioned in the act, the award is purely for Crawley itself (see HRO 38M48/181 for the text and 6M63/12 for the map of this enclosure).

6 *Sussex*

1. WSRO PAR196/20; QDD/6/W7.
2. ESRO TD/E85.
3. ESRO TD/E57.
4. As against the 101 quoted in Chapman and Seeliger, 1995. Doubts exist about the precise number of separate systems in the Chichester-Oving area.
5. No attempt was made to pinpoint precise dates before 1700.
6. Subsequent research has doubled the number known to have survived since the publication of Chapman and Seeliger, 1995 (see p.89).
7. Excluding village greens, and the remnant

Ashdown Forest. Their decision has been followed in dubious cases.

8. For example, there is a specific reference to a common meadow at West Firle as 'the Brooke of Heighton' (WSRO SAS/Box1/14), while Littlehampton Brooks were pasture.

9. PRO IR29/35/3.

10. WSRO Add Ms 18557; PRO IR29/35/66.

11. WSRO QDD/6/W41.

12. Since votes were based on property, dividing the common might increase holding sizes sufficiently to enfranchise additional electors, whose political allegiance was critical.

13. WSRO Raper Box 15. The copy is not totally complete.

14. WSRO QDD/6/W32.

15. WSRO QDD/W41.

16. In view of the small acreages, these have been grouped by 20 year period, rather than by decade.

17. WSRO Ep. VI/27.

18. The circumstances are not entirely clear, but it was normal for the tithe allotments to be fenced at the general expense.

19. ESRO SAS Acc 158.

20. In neither of the latter cases could an actual agreement be found, but there are references in other sources.

21. Brandon, 1963, p. 364; CRO SEAS 689.

22. ESRO Add. Ms.3430.

23. WSRO Petworth 36510.

24. WSRO TD/W123.

25. Three seem to have covered only meadow.

26. WSRO Add Ms 22133 and PAR 212/7/1).

27. WSRO Add Ms 24462.

28. WSRO Goodwood E1159-1181. See Chapman and Seeliger (1995) pp 92-3.

29. WSRO Add Ms 9474 and 1187; TD/W20.

30. PRO IR29/ and IR30/35/70.

31. WSRO Add Ms 28942; TD/W120; PHA 3395-6.

32. ESRO Add Ms 1016.

33. ESRO SAS G17/31.

34. ESRO Add. Mss. 1208.

35. ESRO SAS/Box2/415 and /470.

36. ESRO Adams Ms 46.

37. ESRO SAS/Box20/183.

38. WSRO Add Ms 24462.

39. ESRO SAT C494.

40. ESRO TD/E101.

41. ESRO Adams Ms 51.

42. WSRO Add Ms 9474 and TD/W20.

43. CRO Raper Box CCCC.

6. WRO 212B/3732, Kerridge, 1967, p. 217, V.C.H. XII, pp. 134-5,

7. His son of the same name was even more active.

8. Two others appear also to have survived.

9. See, for example, Whitsbury, which was in Wiltshire at the time of the enclosure (HRO 43M68/PZ1)

10. V.C.H., IX, pp. 70-1

11. WRO 2057/I/7

12. Low banks. WRO E.A.29.

13. WRO E.A.41.

14. WRO E.A.38/5, E.A.115, E.A.111.

15. WCA W54/2/23.

16. Michael Turner, personal communication.

17. WRO E.A.38/4; VCH, XIII, pp. 44-8.

18. PRO IR29/ and IR30/38/32.

19. Michael Turner, personal communication. It is not always clear whether the bills covered identical areas within the parishes concerned.

20. HCJ, 64, p. 79.

21. WCA W54/6/11 (E.B. 12).

22. WRO E.A.167.

23. WRO E.A.75.

24. There was an earlier genuine formal agreement of 1611.

25. WMR/Longbridge Deverill/404 and /409

26. 21 to 11 and 20 to 11 respectively.

27. Brixton Deverill has full details of the acreages allotted and is included here, whereas it is not possible to disentangle the quantities of each type of land from the award.

28. WMR/LD/410.

29. HRO 8M49/T68; WRO E.A.171.

30. HRO 19M61/2145-2147.

31 Paring and burning.

32. WRO 383/298.

33. WRO 212B/3732.

34. For comparison, an incomplete search found 13 informal field enclosures for the seventeenth century.

35. WRO D1/24/25/6.

36. Completed in 1866.

7.Wiltshire

1. HRO 8M49/T68.

2. WRO 490/1007.

3. see V.C.H., 12, pp. 33-35 for an example at Ramsbury.

4. WRO 9/14/48, 9/5/19-20, agree 1703 (not found), 9/8/27, E.A.68, E.A.99,

5. WRO D1/24/119/1-4; D1/24/236/1-3

Bibliography

Afton, B. (1993), 'Mixed farming on the Hampshire Downs, 1837-1914', unpublished PhD thesis, Reading University, pp. 122, 203.

Albery, W. (1927) *A Parliamentary History of the Ancient Borough of Horsham, 1295-1885*, London.

Albery, W. (1947) *A Millenium of Facts in the History of Horsham and Sussex, 947-1947*, Horsham.

Allen, R. C. (1982) 'Efficiency and the Distributional Consequences of Eighteenth Century Enclosures', *Economic Journal*, 92, p.948

Baker, A. H. R. (1963) 'The Field Systems of Kent', unpubl. Ph.D. thesis, University of London.

Baker, A. R. H. and Butlin, R. A. (1973) *Studies of Field Systems in the British Isles*, Cambridge: University Press.

Beresford, M. W. and Hurst, J.G. (1971) *Deserted Medieval Villages*, Lutterworth.

Beresford, M. W. (1948) 'Glebe Terriers and Open Field Leicestershire' in W.G. Hoskins, ed., *Studies in Leicestershire Agrarian History*, Leicester, pp.77-126.

Brandon, P. F. (1963) 'The Common Lands and Wastes of Sussex', unpubl. Ph.D., University of London.

Chapman, J (1976) 'Parliamentary Enclosure in the Uplands: the case of the North York Moors', *Agricultural History Review*, 24, pp.1-17.

Chapman, J. (1977) 'Land Purchasers at Enclosure: evidence from West Sussex', *Local Historian*, 12, pp. 337-341.

Chapman, J. (1978) The Common Lands of Portsea Island', Portsmouth Papers, 29.

Chapman, J. (1980) 'The Parliamentary Enclosures of West Sussex', *Southern History*, 2, pp.73-91.

Chapman, J. (1982) 'The unofficial enclosure proceedings: a study of the Horsham (Sussex) enclosure, 1812-13', *Sussex Archaeological Collections*, 120, pp.185-191.

Chapman, J. (1987) 'The Extent and Nature of Parliamentary Enclosure', *Agricultural History Review*, 35, pp.25-35.

Chapman, J. (1992) 'Efficiency in Land Redistribution: the Case of the English Enclosure Movement', in A.Verhoeve and J.A.J.Vervloet (eds) *The Transformation of the European Rural Landscape: Methodological issues and agrarian change 1770-1914*, Brussels, pp.181-189.

Chapman, J. and Harris, T. M. (1982) 'The accuracy of enclosure estimates: some evidence from Northern England', *Journal of Historical Geography*, 8, pp.261-264.

Chapman, J. and Seeliger, S. (1995) 'Open Fields and their Disappearance in the Eighteenth and Nineteenth Centuries: The Evidence from Sussex', *Southern History*, 17, pp.88-97.

Chapman, J. and Seeliger, S. (1998), *A Guide to Enclosure in Hampshire 1700-1900*, 1998, Hampshire Record Series, No. 15, Winchester

Chapman, J. and Seeliger, S. (1995) 'Formal agreements and the enclosure process: the Evidence from Hampshire' in *Agricultural History Review*, 43 (1), pp.35-46.

Clark. G. (1998) 'Commons Sense: Common Property Rights, Efficiency, and Institutional Change', *Journal of Economic History*, 58, p.92.

Clark, G. (1999) 'In Defense of Commons Sense', *Journal of Economic History*, 59, pp.451-455.

Cohen, J. S. and Weitzman, M. L. (1975) 'Enclosures and Depopulation: a Marxian analysis', in Parker, W.N. and Jones, E.L. (eds) *European Peasants and their Markets,* Princeton, pp.161-178.

Endacott, G. B. (1938) 'The Progress of Enclosures in the County of Dorset in the eighteenth and part of the nineteenth centuries', unpub. B Litt., University of Oxford.

Gilbert, K. (1992), *Life in a Hampshire Village: The History of Ashley*, Hampshire County Council, Winchester.

Gonner, E. C. K. (1912) *Common Land and Inclosure*, London, (reprinted 1966).

Hammond, J. L. and B. (1911) *The Village Labourer*, London.

Ham, J. (1987) *Storrington in Georgian and Victorian Times*, Storrington: Private.

Hoskins, W. G. and Stamp, L. D. (1963) *The Common Lands of England and Wales*, London: Collins.

Hunt, H. G. (1955) 'The Parliamentary Enclosure Movement in Leicestershire 1730-1842', Ph.D. University of London.

Jones, E. L. (1958) 'The arable depression after the Napoleonic Wars and the agricultural development of the Hampshire Chalklands', unpublished B.A. thesis, University of Nottingham.

Kain, R. J. P. and Prince, H. C. (1985) *The Tithe Surveys of England and Wales*, Cambridge University Press.

Kain, R. J. P. and Oliver, R. R. (1995) *The Tithe Maps of England and Wales*, Cambridge: University Press.

Kay, J. E. (1979) 'The Broyle Enclosure, 1767-71', unpublished typescript, ESRO L/Sx 50.

Leconfield, Lord (1954) *Petworth Manor in the Seventeenth Century*, Oxford University Press.

Mee, Rev. J. H. (1913) *Bourne in the Past, being a History of the Parish of Westbourne*, Hove: Combridge's.

Mingay, G. E. (1997) *Parliamentary Enclosure in England*, London: Longman.

Nightingale, M. D. (1952) 'Some Evidence of Open Field Agriculture in Kent', unpubl. B.Litt. thesis, University of Oxford.

Neeson, J. M. (1978) 'Common Right and Enclosure in Eighteenth Century Northamptonshire', Ph. D. University of Warwick.

Neeson, J. M. (1993) *Commoners: common right, enclosure and social change in England, 1700-1820*, Cambridge University Press.

Routh, M. (1986) *Amport, the Story of a Hampshire Parish*, published privately by the author.

Sandell, R. E. (1971) *Abstracts of Wiltshire inclosure awards and agreements*, Wiltshire Records Society, vol 25 for 1969.

Smail, H. (1949) *The Worthing Pageant: the Worthing Map Story*, Worthing: Aldridge Bros.

Tate, W. E. (1943 and 1947) 'A Handlist of Hampshire Inclosure Acts and Awards', *Proceedings of the Hampshire Field Club and Archaeological Society*, 15, pp. 292-296, and 16, pp.257-279.

Tate, W. E. (1944) 'A Handlist of Wiltshire Inclosure Acts and Awards', *Transactions of the Wiltshire Archaeological Society*, 10, pp.127-173.

Tate, W. E. (1950) 'A Handlist of Sussex Inclosure Acts and Awards', *Record Publication*, no. 1, Lewes and Chichester: East and West Sussex County Councils.

Taylor, C. (1970) *Dorset: The Making of the English Landscape*, London: Hodder and Stoughton.

Thirsk, J. (1964), 'The Common Fields', *Past and Present*, 29, pp.3-25.

Thirsk, J. ed. (1967) *The Agrarian History of England and Wales, IV: 1500-1640*, Cambridge: University Press, pp.ix-x.

Thompson, E. P. (1966) *The Making of the English Working Class*, New York, p.218.

Turner, M. E. (1973) 'Some social and economic considerations of Parliamentary enclosure in Buckinghamshire, 1738-1865', Ph.D. University of Sheffield.

Turner, M. E. ed. (1978) *A Domesday of English enclosure acts and awards by W.E.Tate*, Reading University.

Turner, M. E. (1980) *English Parliamentary Enclosures*, Folkestone: Dawson.

Turner, Michael and Wray, Trevor (1991) 'A Survey of Sources for Parliamentary Enclosure: the House of Commons Journal and Commissioners' Working Papers', *Archives*, 19, pp.257-288.

Vancouver, C. (1810), *A General View of the Agriculture of Hampshire*, London.

Young, A. (1908) *General Report on Enclosures*, London: Board of Agriculture

Appendix

Parliamentary enclosures

'Code' is the enclosure number assigned by the National Enclosure Project. 'Acreage' includes all land affected by the award. For Hampshire and Sussex totals were produced by addition of allotments, except for those in italics, which are estimates. Dorset and Wiltshire totals are the best estimates available to the authors.

Awards marked with a star represent acts which were purely confirmatory of an existing agreement.

Code	Act	Award	Acreage	
DORSET				
			Best Est.	
10001	Abbotsbury	1808	1814	1327
10002	Arne	1836	1848	314
10003	Ashmore	1857	1860	642
10004	Askerswell	1845	1854	634.52
10005	Batcombe	1861	1863	393.02
10006	Beaminster	1803	1809	526
10007	Beer Hackett	1836	1853	140.17
10008	Belchalwell	1836	1854	70.34
10009	Bere Regis	1836	1846	1756.08
10010	Bincombe	1824	1828	878
10011	Bradford Peverell	1797	1798	660
10012	Briantspuddle (Affpuddle)	1836	1839	167
10013	Broadmayne	1804	1811	709
10014	Buckland Newton	1733	1734	1482
10015	Buckland Newton	1849	1854	283
10016	Canford Magna	1805	1822	11043
10017	Cann	1809	1812	217
10018	Cattistock	1807	1816	905
10019	Caundle Marsh	1836	1845	72
10021	Charlton Marshall	1798	1800	2049.21
10020	Charminster	1830	1837	651
10023	Cheselbourne	1836	1845	459.09
10024	Chickerell	1789	1792	111
10022	Chickerell	1803	1804	560
10025	Child Okeford	1836	1847	288
10026	Chilfrome	1820	1820	882
10027	Church Knowle	1853	1856	153
10028	Compton Abbas	1851	1853	708
10029	Compton Valence	1808	1809	1122
10030	Corfe Mullen	1807	1815	2017
10031	Corscombe	1815	1818	108
10032	Cranborne	1856	1858	842
10033	Cranborne Chase (Dorset)	1828	1829	11443.87
10034	Dewlish	1815	1820	380
10035	Edmondsham	1802	1806	740
10036	Farnham	1836	1850	235
10037	Fontmell Magna	1845	1853	358
10038	Gillingham	1809	?	500
10039	Godmanstone	1836	1840	565

10040	Gussage St Michael	1812	1816	1030
10041	Hampreston	1806	1813	4090
10042	Handley, Sixpenny	1795	1797	716
10043	Hazelbury Bryan	1836	1858	151
10044	Hinton Martell	1797	1798	1743
10045	Holwell	1797	1799	482.72
10046	Iwerne Minster	1836	1854	601
10047	Knighton, West	1779	1785	1009
10048	Langton Herring	1760	1762	954
10049	Leigh	1798	1804	640
10050	Litton Cheyney	1809	1812	611
10055	Lulworth, East	1761	*1761	1357.57
10051	Lulworth, West	1855	1857	1188
10057	Lydlinch	1864	1867	75
10052	Lytchett Matravers	1818	1829	3067
10053	Maiden Newton	1830	1835	730
10054	Margaret Marsh	1859	1862	13
10060	Mappowder	1798	1807	315.76
10056	Marnhull	1859	1862	81
10058	Morden	1768	1769	973
10059	Mosterton	1845	1854	44
10061	Orchard, East	1861	1865	23
10062	Owermoigne	1829	1846	1179
10063	Piddlehinton	1831	1835	1116
10064	Piddletrenthide	1815	1817	2349
10065	Pimperne	1808	1814	2175
10066	Plush	1808	1825	346
10069	Portesham	1762	1764	649
10068	Powerstock	1811	1812	322
10067	Powerstock	1861	1863	423
10070	Preston	1793	1798	1485
10071	Radipole	1604	none	negligible
10072	Rampisham	1813	1817	800
10073	Shapwick(e)	1810	1813	1177
10074	Sherborne	1836	1849	242
10075	Silton	1860	1862	77
10076	Spetisbury	1803	1809	1063
10077	Stafford, West	1736	1736	553
10078	Stalbridge	1811	1819	466
10079	Stoke, East	1868	1870	476
10080	Stour, East	1803	1804	293
10081	Stourpaine	1851	1860	1530
10082	Stour, West	1779	none	200
10087	Sturminster Marshall	1836	1845	1616
10083	Sturminster Newton	1824	1830	433.48
10088	Sturminster Newton	1836	1844	95
10084	Sydling St Nicholas	1819	1824	2475
10085	Tarrant Hinton	1823	1827	1039
10086	Tarrant Keynston	1814	*none	169
10093	Tolpuddle	1793	1794	537.68
10089	Trent	1836	1852	273.96
10095	Turnworth	1801	1805	531.20
10090	Up Loders	1817	1821	361
10091	Upwey	1834	1839	330
10092	Walditch	1809	1813	208
10094	Wareham	1861	1866	554
10100	Warmwell	1866	1868	598.32
10096	Wimborne Minster	1784	1786	2671
10097	Winfrith Newburgh	1768	1771	2144
10098	Winterborne Abbas	1808	1810	608
10099	Winterborne Kingston	1836	1848	1255.93
10101	Winterborne Monkton	1808	1808	622
10102	Winterborne Steepleton	1861	1863	832
10103	Winterborne St(r)ickland	1799	1802	1050
10104	Wool	1837	1839	853
10105	Wootton Glanvilles	1852	1855	28

10106	Wyke Regis	1794	1798	645
	TOTAL			103137.92

HAMPSHIRE

				Total
14001	Abbotts Ann	1774	1775	1844.86
14002	Aldershot	1853	1856	2408.04
14003	Alresford, New	1805	1807	345.54
14004	Alresford, Old	1736	1737	634.96
14005	Alresford, Old	1803	1805	104.43
14006	Alverstoke	1887	1888	*5*
14008	Andover	1740	*none	*350*
14007	Andover	1783	1785	2905.54
14009	Baddesley,North	1857	1867	725.33
14010	Barton Stacey	1757	*none	2487.32
14011	Basing	1796	1797	482.29
14012	Basingstoke	1786	1788	3387.51
14013	Bentley	1851	1859	222.31
14014	Bere, Forest of	1810	1814	492.31
14015	Binsted	1849	1857	1156.11
14016	Bishopstoke	1820	1825	452.87
14017	Bishopstoke	1853	1857	180.63
14018	Boldre	1811	1820	637.61
14019	Botley	1859	1865	81.15
14020	Bourne, St Mary	1815	See text	2536.84
14021	Broughton	1789	1790	3009.41
14022	Burghclere	1757	?	597
14023	Buriton	1854	1864	915.28
14024	Buriton	1855	1861	39.86
14025	Bursledon	1854	1857	236.91
14026	Chalton	1812	1816	3258.87
14028	Chilbolton	1836	1838	1634.22
14029	Chawton	1741	*1741	629.65
14027	Chilworth	1857	1867	11.73
14030	Christchurch	1802	1805	5226.9
14114	Christchurch	1825	1827	417.84
14031	Christchurch	1868	1878	271.36
14032	Clatford, Lower	1854	1855	81.8
14933	Clatford, Upper	1785	1786	1292.32
14034	Colemore	1808	none	650
14035	Cove	1854	1859	1120.83
14036	Crawley	1794	1795	2002.6
14037	Crondall	1847	1849	62.94
14038	Crookham	1829	1834	3277.23
14039	Curdridge	1854	1856	294.78
14040	Damerham, South	1818	1830	1687.36
14041	Dibden	1790	1791	454.31
14042	Dibden	1859	1862	335.61
14043	Droxford	1851	1855	1198.98
14044	Dummer	1743	1744	1688.33
14045	Durley	1856	1858	117.65
14046	Easton	1799	1800	1089.58
14047	Ecchinswell	1813	1815	580.98
14048	Ecchinswell	1816	1819	804.6
14049	Eling	1810	1814	2573.32
14050	Ellingham	1822	1827	478.57
14052	Ellisfield	1848	1851	141.41
14051	Elvetham	1813	1815	1881.94
14053	Eversley	1864	1868	1148.55
14054	Fareham	1805	1807	421.19
14057	Farnborough	1811	1816	1289.49
14055	Fawley	1813	1815	362.94
14056	Fordingbridge	1863	1865	12.67

14058	Froxfield	1803	1805	760.39
14059	Grateley	1778	1778	504.78
14060	Greatham	1848	1851	74.54
14061	Hambledon	1852	1862	182.38
14062	Hambledon	1852	1857	484.39
14063	Hambledon	1865	1871	326.33
14064	Hambledon	1865	1870	77.77
14065	Harbridge	1817	1817	371.11
14066	Hartley Wintney	1865	1867	30.01
14067	Havant	1864	1870	891.4
14068	Hayling, North	1836	1840	173.81
14069	Hayling, North	1836	1840	206.76
14072	Hayling, North	1836	1867	189.93
14105	Hayling, North	1836	1867	90.96
14070	Hayling, North	1840	1874	31.23
14071	Hayling, North	1840	1876	58.63
14075	Headbourne Worthy	1788	1791	1650.09
14076	Headley	1849	1859	1542.61
14073	Heckfield	1858	1861	563.65
14074	Highclere	1781	1783	2225.3
14112	Hill and Shirley	1829	1832	356.29
14113	Houghton	1794	1795	851.31
14077	Hursley	1809	1813	2566.56
14078	Hurstbourne Tarrant	1818	1820	826.48
14079	Itchen Abbas	1812	1812	185.12
14080	Kilmeston	1803	1805	797.29
14081	Kingsclere	1842	1845	2584.68
14082	Leckford	1780	1780	1813.71
14083	Liss	1856	1864	662.25
14084	Littleton	1843	1844	1269.22
14085	Lockerley	1811	1815	251.86
14086	Longparish	1802	1804	860.9
14087	Mapledurwell	1856	1863	98.59
14088	Medstead	1798	1799	746.73
14089	Meon, East	1856	1859	122.93
14090	Meonstoke	1856	1863	676.1
14091	Michelmersh	1796	1797	982.73
14092	Milton	1860	1862	153.62
14093	Monxton	1806	1807	778.72
14094	Morestead	1852	1852	153.56
14095	Newton Vallence	1848	1850	166.43
14096	Odiham	1739	*none	*25*
14097	Odiham	1798	1791	1781.24
14098	Otterbourne	1836	1837	59.34
14099	Ovington	1812	1813	877.12
14100	Owslebury	1851	1861	1043.3
14101	Oxenbourn	1839	1851	776.5
14102	Pamber	1824	1827	1049.46
14103	Petersfield	1857	1859	6.56
14104	Portchester	1808	1809	804.19
14106	Portsea	1785	1786	357.82
14107	Portsea	1810	1813	180.06
14108	Portsea	1817	1822	151.22
14109	Preston Candover	1820	1823	2118.62
14110	Preston Candover	1866	1870	177.21
14111	Quarley	1794	1795	696.56
14138	Ringwood	1807	1811	2639.23
14116	Ringwood	1864	1868	2521.31
14117	Rockbourne	1798	1802	1575.44
14115	Romsey Extra	1804	1808	2600.13
14118	Ropley	1709	none	500
14119	Rotherwick	1849	1859	158.28
14121	Selbourne	1866	1868	177.76
14122	Sheet	1855	1859	268.56
14120	Sherborne,Monk	1792	1793	711.9
14123	Sherbourne, Monk	1829	1832	194.63

14126	Sherbourne St John	1829	1832	1406.82
14127	Sherfield English	1806	1810	167
14124	Shipton Bellinger	1792	1793	1318.12
14125	Soberton	1858	1867	450.81
14128	Sombourne,Kings	1783	1784	2087.08
14129	Sopley	1864	1869	1202.39
14130	Southampton	1844	none	*25*
14131	Steep	1856	1866	146.04
14132	Stoneham, North	1744	⋆none	604
14133	Stoneham, South	1812	1814	794.09
14134	Stoneham, South	1813	1815	1553.46
14135	Stratfield Turgis	1853	1866	178.86
14136	Tadley	1847	1850	661.39
14137	Tangley	1827	?	95
14139	Titchfield	1859	1866	832.77
14140	Titchfield	1859	1867	12.78
14141	Titchfield	1859	1867	38.23
14142	Titchfield	1859	1866	267.04
14143	Twyford	1851	1855	858.94
14144	Upham	1852	1860	229.48
14145	Upton Grey	1794	1796	349.22
14146	Wallop, Nether	1796	1797	2192.51
14148	Wallop, Upper	1786	1787	3119.48
14149	Waltham, Bishops	1759	1760	196.07
14150	Waltham, Bishops	1863	1870	144.6
14147	Warblington	1810	1814	519.57
14151	Wellow, East	1730	none	*100*
14152	Wellow, West	1809	1811	360.81
14153	Weyhill	1812	1818	872.11
14154	Whitchurch	1797	1798	1638.16
14155	Wolverton	1857	1861	33.76
14156	Woodhay, East	1749	⋆none	1300
14157	Woolmer Forest	1858	1868	1186.62
14158	Wootton St Lawrence	1829	1832	208.22
14159	Worthy, Kings	1845	1852	479.73
14160	Wymering	1812	1815	492.16
14161	Yateley	1815	1817	1763.1
36014	Warblington (area in Hants)			127.82
	TOTAL			139545.49

EAST SUSSEX

				Total
35001	Ashdown Forest	1884	1887	305.31
35002	Bexhill	1895	1896	45.17
35003	Chailey	1841	1842	312.8
35004	Clayton	1852	1857	94.17
35005	Cuckfield	1858	1862	159.65
35006	Eastbourne	1845	1853	632.72
35007	Framfield	1856	1862	1884.77
35008	Hailsham	1849	1855	130.14
35009	Horsted Keynes	1860	1864	196.51
35010	Keymer	1828	1829	464.14
35011	Kingston	1830	1830	2332.3
35012	Laughton	1813	1818	1765.77
35013	Piecombe	1869	1872	306.14
35014	Portslade	1859	1861	383.58
35015	Ringmer	1767	1769	1949.44
35016	Rye	1833	1838	748.09
35017	Southease	1836	1844	783.89
35018	Telscombe	1810	1811	454.75
35019	Wivelsfield	1859	1861	34.36
	TOTAL			12983.7

WEST SUSSEX

				Total
36001	Aldingbourne	1777	1777	406.84
36002	Amberley	1810	1828	2085.13
36003	Angmering	1809	1812	319.47
36004	Ashington	1813	1816	331.94
36005	Ashington	1847	1851	264.56
36006	Barnham	1845	1853	81.54
36007	Bepton	1833	1834	109.31
36008	Birdham	1791	1793	355.42
36009	Bosham	1821	1834	998.38
36010	Boxgrove	1848	1856	62.92
36011	Broadwater	1805	1810	935.73
36012	Bury	1841	1854	1948.12
36013	Chidham	1809	1812	543.30
36014	Chidham	1819	1821	226.26
36015	Chiltington, West	1857	1868	102.04
36016	Chiltington, West	1857	1868	107.32
36017	Chithurst	1859	1862	225.64
36018	Durrington	1814	1818	529.54
36019	Eartham	1813	1817	1269.57
36020	Elsted	1797	1801	272.24
36021	Felpham	1826	?	461.98
36022	Findon	1845	1856	657.91
36023	Goring	1804	1805	407.71
36024	Grinstead,West	1868	1872	87.31
36025	Horsham	1812	1813	750.03
36027	Horsham	1854	1858	13.22
36026	Horsham	1857	1858	21.09
36028	Houghton	1799	1809	1469.74
36029	Hunston	1868	1871	72.18
36030	Hunston	1869	1872	15.83
36031	Ifield	1853	1855	60.27
36032	Iping	1854	1857	231.44
36033	Lancing	1803	1805	818.45
36034	Lavant, East	1848	1856	94.90
36035	Lavant, Mid	1848	1856	93.31
36036	Littlehampton	1836	1841	162.34
36037	Lyminster	1804	1805	171.16
36038	Nuthurst	1865	1871	29.36
36039	Oving	1845	1849	157.93
36040	Poling	1812	1813	275.67
36041	Pulborough	1808	1815	291.66
36042	Pulborough	1850	1855	181.79
36043	Pulborough	1855	1857	19.39
36044	Rogate	1820	1825	900.14
36045	Rogate	1856	1861	832.12
36046	Rudgewick	1851	1851	30.16
36047	Rustington	1803	1805	409.22
36048	Rustington	1836	1839	39.83
36049	Selsey	1819	1830	696.35
36050	Sidlesham	1785	1792	217.02
36051	Slindon	1864	1870	956.89
36052	Southwick	1856	1858	128.86
36053	Storrington	1850	1858	226.38
36054	Stoughton	1861	1863	279.23
36055	Tangmere	1821	?	202.40
36056	Tarring, West	1808	1811	465.66
36057	Terwick	1858	1861	106.39
36058	Thakeham	1808	1812	293.47
36059	Thorney, West	1812	1818	973.79
36060	Walberton	1769	1769	239.25
36061	Warningcamp	1809	1812	307.70
36062	Westbourne	1818	1823	774.24
36063	Westbourne	1836	1841	155.26
36064	Westbourne	1857	1859	187.09

36065	Wisborough Green	1858	1864	90.69
36066	Wisborough Green	1861	1871	189.98
36067	Wittering, West	1791	1793	175.14
36068	Woolavington with Graffham	1815	1820	1203.10
	TOTAL			27800.30

WILTSHIRE

				BestEst
41001	Aldbourne	1805	1809	3896
41002	Alderbury	1803	1809	986
41003	All Cannings	1797	1799	3183
41004	Ashton, Steeple	1813	1818	2173
41005	Ashton Keynes	1767	1767	674
41006	Ashton Keynes	1777	1778	1976
41007	Avebury	1792	1795	2307
41008	Badbury	1748	1748	685.02
41009	Barford St Martin	1809	1815	2486
41010	Bedwyn, Great	1790	1792	3467
41011	Bedwyn, Great	1812	1815	734
41012	Berwick St James	1789	1790	1682
41013	Berwick St John	1786	1794	1678
41014	Berwick St Leonard	1818	1840	836
41015	Biddestone St Nicholas	1811	1812	730.76
41016	Bishopstone (N.Wilts)	1809	1813	2700
41017	Bishopstrow	1808	1811	877
41018	Blunsdon St Andrew	1749	1749	885
41019	Boscombe, West	1862	1866	595
41020	Bower Chalke	1855	1860	1182.39
41021	Boyton	1828	1829	2101
41022	Bradford	1818	1821	46
41023	Bradford	1852	1853	180.95
41024	Bradford	1863	1867	9
41025	Bradley, North	1790	1792	483.12
41026	Bradley, North	1804	1807	957.55
41027	Bremhill	1775	1777	389
41028	Brinkworth	1806	1808	561
41029	Broad Chalke	1814	1861	3777
41030	Bromham	1811	1814	221
41031	Calne	1813	1818	1679
41032	Cannings, Bishop's	1778	1780	851
41033	Cannings, Bishop's	1815	1819	2639
41035	Charlton All Saints	1801	1807	1503
41034	Charlton St Peter	1780	1780	1601
41036	Cherhill	1820	1822	1572
41037	Cheverell, Great	1797	1802	2263
41038	Chicklade	1781	1781	971
41039	Chilton Foliat	1809	1813	401
41041	Chippenham	1845	1856	580
41040	Chippenham	1867	1869	51
41042	Chirton	1800	1808	1049
41043	Chirton	1814	1816	647
41044	Chiseldon	1779	1780	1176
41045	Chitterne St Mary	1816	1818	4934
41046	Christian Malford	1836	1843	24
41047	Chute	1808	1820	595
41048	Codford St Mary	1836	1844	1267
41049	Codford St Peter	1808	1810	697
41050	Codford St Peter	1814	1815	693
41051	Colerne	1785	1787	1293
41052	Collingbourne Kingston	1815	1824	1744
41053	Compton Bassett	1725	★none	250
41054	Compton Bassett	1831	1837	63
41055	Coombe Bissett	1802	1806	1955

41056	Corsham	1816	1819	36
41058	Cricklade	1786	1788	705
41057	Cricklade	1814	1824	771
41059	Crudwell	1816	1841	1314.92
41060	Donhead St Mary	1865	1867	535
41062	Downton	1813	1822	2167
41061	Downton	1816	1847	1148.73
41063	Durnford	1793	1795	957
41064	Durnford	1821	1824	782
41065	Easterton	1797	1798	1320
41066	Edington	1854	1865	89
41069	Enford	1770	1772	1008
41067	Enford	1805	1808	2870
41068	Enford	1814	1817	674
41070	Enford	1853	1856	944
41072	Erlestoke	1777	1782	1624
41073	Everley	1816	1782	387.61
41074	Figheldean	1819	1823	3118
41075	Figheldean	1836	1844	1449
41076	Fittleton	1836	1839	918
41077	Fovant	1785	1792	14899
41078	Froxfield	1818	1823	928
41079	Grimstead, East	1836	1849	479
41080	Grimstead, West	1802	1805	584
41081	Ham	1827	1828	1614
41082	Hankerton	1808	1809	522
41083	Heddington	1766	1767	786
41084	Heytesbury	1783	1785	4951
41085	Hilperton	1815	1816	111.83
41086	Highworth	1778	1779	3177
41087	Hinton, Broad	1821	1822	390
41088	Idmiston	1836	1850	887
41089	Keevil	1794	1796	3316
41090	Kingston Deverill	1782	1785	2499
41091	Kington, West	1809	1811	1087
41092	Knook	1792	1798	1450
41093	Knoyle, East	1798	1799	839
41094	Knoyle, East	1865	1867	365
41095	Landford	1858	1861	740
41096	Landford	1858	1860	56
41097	Langford, Steeple	1833	1836	1000
41098	Langford, Steeple	1863	1866	985
41099	Latton-cum-Eisey	1801	1805	1074
41100	Laverstock	1818	1820	1261
41101	Lavington, Market	1777	1781	1995
41102	Lavington, West	1836	1840	4183
41105	Lea	1805	1806	174
41106	Liddington	1776	1777	1002
41103	Littleton Drew	1840	1847	546.47
41104	Longbridge Deverill	1790	1795	2926.60
41107	Ludgershall	1851	1853	87
41108	Maddington	1845	1853	997
41109	Maddington	1852	1855	555
41110	Malmesbury	1819	1831	250
41111	Malmesbury	1821	1832	278
41112	Manningford Bruce	1801	1812	734
41113	Marston Maisey	1864	1866	94
41114	Melksham	1813	1814	505.05
41115	Mere	1807	1821	2977
41116	Mildenhall	1779	*none	478
41117	Milston and Brigmerston	1779	*none	500
41118	Milton Lilbourne	1774	1781	468
41120	Minety	1811	1813	728
41121	Netheravon	1788	1790	3320
41119	Nettleton	1812	1814	530
41122	Newnton, North	1836	1840	205

41123	Norton Bavant	1805	1809	1348
41124	Oaksey	1802	1802	94
41125	Odstock	1783	1787	2550
41126	Ogbourne St Andrew	1778	1780	1286
41127	Patney	1778	1780	604.38
41128	Ogbourne St George	1792	1796	1609
41129	Orcheston St George	1809	1796	695
41130	Overton, West	1814	1821	2691
41131	Pewsey	1775	1777	1387
41132	Pewsey	1825	1826	425
41133	Pitton	1810	1819	1135
41134	Potterne	1824	1835	268
41138	Purton	1732	1733	260
41157	Purton	1737	1738	1000
41137	Purton	1799	1799	421
41135	Ramsbury	1777	1778	2317
41136	Rodborne Cheney	1819	1820	584.28
41140	Roundway	1794	1812	4607
41141	Rushall	1803	1804	103
41142	Seagry	1845	1883	124
41143	Shalbourne	1800	1805	1464
41144	Sherston Magna	1741	1743	1317
41145	Sherston Parva	1840	1844	84
41146	Shrewton	1798	1801	2112
41147	Somerford, Great	1806	1809	1147
41148	Somerford, Little	1790	1792	374
41149	Somerford, Little	1808	?	139
41150	Stanton St Quintin	1782	1783	331
41151	Sta(u)nton	1732	*none	800
41152	Stockton	1809	1818	1732
41153	Stratford sub Castle	1799	1800	1451
41154	Stratton St Margaret	1795	1796	1836
41155	Sutton Mandeville	1814	none	670.11
41156	Sutton Veny	1798	1804	2870.85
41158	Teffont Magna	1822	1837	3671
41159	Tidcombe	1774	1782	811
41160	Tilshead	1811	1814	3632
41161	Tisbury, East	1834	1836	1
41162	Upavon	1802	1804	2380
41163	Upton Lovell	1815	1825	1307
41139	Upton Scudamore	1803	1805	1898.10
41164	Urchfont	1789	1793	1850
41165	Wanborough	1779	1780	3715
41166	Warminster	1780	1783	4668
41167	Westbury	1802	1808	6486
41168	Wilcot	1799	1803	395
41169	Wilsford (Dauntsey)	1801	1808	1602
41170	Wilsford (N. Wilts)	1802	1805	934
41171	Wilton	1825	1860	2706
41172	Wingfield (alias Winkfield)	1822	1823	76
41173	Winterbourne Dauntsey	1848	1851	438
41174	Winterbourne Earls	1795	1796	2344
41175	Winterbourne Gunner	1852	1853	552
41176	Winterbourne Monkton	1813	1815	948
41177	Winterbourne Stoke	1810	1812	4678
41178	Wootton Bassett	1820	1822	72
41179	Wootton Rivers	1836	1842	135
41180	Wroughton (Elstub)	1795	1796	2117.53
41181	Wroughton	1796	1797	1238
41071	Wylye	1836	1861	1352
10033	Cranborne Chase (area in Wilts)			3306.10
	TOTAL			256458.35

Index